To Kevin

"Better Than
Perfect"

Mulkeran

"What have you tried
lately?"

Better than Perfect

Better than Perfect

by

Dale Dauten

How Gifted Bosses and Great Employees
Can Lift the Performance of
Those Around Them

CAREER
PRESS
THE CAREER PRESS, INC.
Franklin Lakes, NJ

BETTER THAN PERFECT
EDITED AND TYPESET BY ASTRID DERIDDER
Cover design by Lu Rossman/Digi Dog Design NYC
Printed in the U.S.A. by Book-mart Press

To order this title, please call toll-free 1-800-CAREER-1 (NJ and Canada: 201-
848-0310) to order using VISA or MasterCard, or for further information on
books from Career Press.

The Career Press, Inc., 3 Tice Road, PO Box 687,
Franklin Lakes, NJ 07417
www.careerpress.com

Library of Congress Cataloging-in-Publication Data

Dauten, Dale A.
    Better than perfect : how gifted bosses and great employees can lift the
performance of those around them / by Dale Dauten
        p. cm.
    Includes bibliographical references and index.
    ISBN-13 *978-1-56414-880-3 (hardcover)
    ISBN-10 1-56414-880-7 (hardcover)
        1. Creative ability in business. 2. Employee motivation. 3. Intrapersonal
        communication. 4. Teams in the workplace. I. Title.

HD53.D377 2006
658.3'14—dc22

                                                            2005058104

For Joel and Jeri

May you live all the days of your life.

—Jonathan Swift

Contents

Preface

"You make me want to be a better man." That grand compliment, spoken by Jack Nicholson in the film *As Good As It Gets*, echoed in my mind as I searched organizations for people who are as good as it gets, for the men and women at every level who are so good at improving their own performance that they end up elevating those around them.

I eventually came to think of these people as 'better than perfect.' Why such an odd and seemingly illogical appellation? To explain, I need to tell you about the time I met the world's greatest flute player, the late Jean-Pierre Rampal. I was living outside Los Angeles when I heard that he would be giving a master class at a college across town. Although I don't play the flute, I decided to attend. So it was that I got to sit in as a dozen prodigies played for the master and listened to his counsel and interpretations of the musical passages. Rampal's versions were sometimes so strikingly different that I asked him how far he was willing to go in experimenting with what the composer had written. He thought for a moment, scowling, and then replied, "There are nights I go out and play a piece *perfectly*. Then—the next night—I play it *better*."

From that day on I began to think of exceptional performance as 'better than perfect.' Moreover, the great ones, the masters, aren't just perfecting their assignments, they are experimenting with their craft, so that just when you thought they were perfect, they surprise you with something even better. Isn't that the essence of genius?

What does it take to be a workplace genius? Having studied hundreds of them, I believe that better-than-perfect colleagues have traits we all have—they simply live them more vividly. That's why I believe it is important to tell their stories and celebrate their work lives—to remind us of the best of ourselves.

We come into the workplace determined to make a difference, to be special, to contribute our talents and be recognized for them. Slowly, those grand aspirations get worn away by what Shakespeare called "the rough torrent of occasion." We work hard, we fit in; somewhere we forget that each of us goes to work entrusted with the jewels of humanity.

So, with this book I invite you to join me in celebrating great executives, employees, suppliers, and customers. Doing so, let us not only learn from them, but also to remember the best of ourselves.

———————

To convey the lessons in a format that I hope is readable and memorable, I have once again called upon business genius Max Elmore to be our guide, this time inviting his nephew to be our narrator for a three-way conversation.

Introduction

The Company Jewels

What I'm looking for is a blessing that's not in disguise.
                                    —Kitty O'Neill Collins

Before I was a genius, I was a drudge.
                                    —Ignace Jan Paderewski

———————————————

"Oh, just come on," I insisted. "It'll cheer you up. And *I'll buy.*"

Angelina, my girlfriend and semi-fiancée, hesitated but didn't bite. "If you buy dinner, that'll just make things *worse*," she countered. "You'll be Mr. Peppy and I'll be lousy company and eventually I'll feel so guilty I'll have to pretend to laugh at your stories."

"Hmmm. Understood. So, here's Plan B. I'll pick up some Chinese food, charge it to *your* Visa card, and you can sulk all you want. And I promise to be glum. Quietly, grimly glum. Picture a mime at a Republican funeral."

"No, I can't picture that—for one thing, mimes aren't Republicans. There's no money in it."

"Oh, sure, that's what most people think. But that's only because the big-time mimes—the ones who know the secret to making serious money—*aren't talking.*"

I could near her stifle a chuckle by turning it into a cough. "Back to your offer, which was, 'I pay and you'll be glum.' That's the deal?"

"Maybe I'll bring a depressing movie. Did you see *House of Sand and Fog?*"

"You had me at glum."
"Deal. Mongolian beef, pot stickers…"
"And sizzling rice soup."
"I'll be there in half an hour."

———————————

Just a little light conversation, but it's as good a place as any to start our story. I'm good at cheering people up; after all, as a sales guy, I'm a monster of cheerfulness.

The reason that Angelina was in need of pepping up that evening was that she'd had lunch that day with a high school friend who'd just gotten a big promotion at the giant corporation where she works. Isn't that a marvelous expression—a *big promotion*? It suggests that you didn't just step up to a new title, but leapt up. Angelina had been forced that day to confront the fact that she had never known that leaping feeling. I hadn't, either.

As we were eating our Chinese food, we talked about the most successful people we'd worked with and what it was that made them different. We weren't getting far. That's when I threw out a suggestion: "We could go visit my uncle and talk it over with him. He's always telling me how he wants to meet you. He'd have some ideas for us. The old guy is a genius. Really."

She was skeptical, and I don't blame her. Meeting my parents had been an ordeal for her. It was different with my uncle, though; Angelina had heard me brag about my uncle Max. I'd also given her articles about him in business magazines.

"What's he like?" she asked, and I knew we'd be meeting him soon.

"He has this quiet power about him, like, oh, maybe a Robert Duvall. You know how Duvall has a dignity about him, but you still get glimpses of something boyish? With Max, he's corny and proud of it. And he'll be crazy about you. I want to show you off to him."

That finished the deliberations.

I called Max from her condo and he was, as anticipated, delighted to hear that I wanted to visit him. After some calendar roulette, we found a couple of days when we all could meet and he said, "I'm sending you tickets. A driver will meet you at the airport."

"Tickets to where?"

"Wherever I'll be—probably Phoenix. It depends on a client of mine. But I'll send tickets, via e-mail. And don't worry, because I'll get the hotel."

I thanked him, but he nimbly cut me off and changed the subject. "Okay, get this Angela on the line. I have questions for her."

"It's Ange*lina*. And this phone has a speakerphone, unless it's secret."

"Ha!" was all he said. So I pushed the button and introduced Max to Angelina. And right away he started in with questions. Eventually Max got to the point of our planned visit: "My nephew tells me that our get-together will include a discussion of work, which happens to be my favorite subject. In fact, I'm a collector of wisdom about work. For instance, I just added a marvelously inappropriate quote to my collection. It's from Homer Simpson: 'If something goes wrong, blame the guy who doesn't speak any English.'"

He laughed his big laugh, and then asked, "Does that one happen to solve your problem?"

After giggling, Angelina said, "Well..." reluctance slowing her voice. "That's just it, I'm not sure there's a problem. I have a good job at a good company. What made me think that I'm missing something is visiting my friend from school, who is this giant star where she works. But I can't figure out why. I mean, she's my friend and I love her to death, *but...*" The final word had a shrug in it. "I can't decide if she's just lucky or what. Every time I try to do something to really stand out at work, the whole effort seems to just drift away and I end up doing the same-old, same-old."

Max replied by saying, "Ah, yes! Like in *The Great Gatsby*, 'So we beat on. Boats against the current, being borne ceaselessly into the past.' Isn't that just how life goes? The currents of life pull us back to the ordinary. We want to be travelers to a distant shore, and then the relentlessness of life pulls us back."

Neither of us knew what to say in response to that. Max did however, suddenly adding, "Wait. Better yet. It's like that Stephen Spender poem:

> *"What I had not foreseen*
> *was the gradual day*
> *weakening the will*
> *leaking the brightness away."*

After a small pause, Max asked, "Does that sound like what you're talking about—the gradual day?"

I grinned at Angelina as she shook her head in admiration, then I told Max, "That's exactly what I was going to say. You took the words out of my mouth."

He gave one of his honking laughs and said, "You and I are more alike than you realize, my young smart-aleck. But here's what I'm leading up to—a big goal for you both. Ready?"

We both agreed.

"The other day I heard the expression 'a handful of jewels.' And it hit me that I was hearing a description of what it is that good companies have—they have a handful of jewels. You with me?"

I shrugged at Angelina but ventured that we *might* be following him.

"You know that cliché executives use?" Max continued. "The one about 'employees are our most important resource'? It's true, but it doesn't ring true, if you know what I mean.

"Unfortunately, the reason the saying doesn't ring true is because everyone knows that nearly all the employees could be replaced within a few weeks and the company would not be affected. But the key word in that sentence is *nearly*. Not all the employees, but *nearly* all the employees.

"Every good company has a few special people who work to create an organization that is special, both to its customers and its employees. And they can show up at any level of the organization, and sometimes outside of it—a special supplier or consultant."

I could hear a faint clicking and I knew he was tapping the table for emphasis as he added, "Those few special people are what makes the company special. Sure, there may be a patent or formula that makes the company's products different, but where did those ideas come from? From that handful of people who aren't just special, but who are contagious, carriers of an epidemic of specialness."

The Assignment

He paused to give us time to respond, but we each waited for the other. Eventually Angelina said, "That's an appealing notion, but

I'm trying to think of who in my company might fit that description. We don't have any perfect employees."

"Perfect, eh? Well, you have a raised an interesting issue: What's a *perfect* colleague like, whether a boss, an employee, a supplier, or a customer? That question has brought us to one of the great secrets of business: *better than perfect*. That sounds impossible, but I've worked with plenty of companies that are so obsessed with avoiding mistakes that they miss opportunities. The same idea holds true for colleagues as well; we are *intimidated* by perfect people, but *inspired* by better-than-perfect people."

Max paused and then said, "Angelina, I bet that if you give up looking for perfect and look for better than perfect, you can spot a jewel among the people you work with. In fact, let's make that your assignment for when we meet. But don't look in your own department—they may be too close for you to be objective about—look among the other departments and among your suppliers or customers to find those people who make the company special."

"I'll do it," said Angelina. "Absolutely." And I knew she would.

But I wanted to get in on it, too, and so I said, "Hey, count me in for this jewel hunt!"

Max interrupted me with a happy bark. "The jewel hunt! I'll remember that one. That would lead to a good name for headhunters—the jewel thieves! But back to the point, which is that I'm delighted you want to join in. I'll be eager to hear what you learn. When I see you, I'm going to ask you for your best find on your hunt. Deal?"

We agreed, of course, at which point Max said, "My assignment for the jewel hunt will be to talk with people I admire about people they admire and see what I come up with. I've got lots of calls to make."

I could tell that his mind was racing off, plotting his research strategy. That was like Max, always generous with his time, money, and talents. However, given that he was already planning to meet with us, and even pay our way to visit him, I felt he was offering to do too much and I said so.

"Ah, here's where you peek behind the curtain," he said mysteriously.

Max then explained that he was being given some big award and had to give an acceptance speech and couldn't decide on a topic to talk about.

"You, my young nephew, have handed me a topic—and you two have been snookered into doing research. You think I'm being generous, but—HA!—you've just been bamboozled into helping me author a speech I believe I will call 'How to be Better than Perfect.'"

News of Max's speech started us joshing about who was helping whom, but when a lull came, I asked for some guidance: "What should we be looking for, specifically?"

"You know me—not much for specifics. And I'm not sure myself yet. I'm going to start by reflecting back on the people who've worked for me who were special. Let me think." He then added in a voice that I recognized as a set-up for one of his old jokes, "You don't know me, Angelina, but I have a photographic memory."

Angelina sounded impressed, but then Max cut in with his punch line: "But it no longer offers same-day service."

"I warned you!" I told Angelina, sighing.

Best-Ever Colleagues

"Okay," Max said, "back to the subject. Let me start by telling you about one of my favorite colleagues, John Ball.

"John made me love my work. When I was planning a project, I'd start thinking about telling John about it. I knew I had to make it unique, to impress him. So before I ever called him, before I ever met with him, just *thinking about his being involved* raised the level of expectation."

"Wait a minute," I interjected. "I met him last time I was at your office. I thought he was a consultant to your company. Isn't he supposed to be figuring out how to impress you?"

"It's not like that with terrific colleagues; it's not the usual org-chart thing. We're talking about people who make you better, so who's leading and who's following? As the Zen master Hekiganroku put it:

> *"The disciple shows his gratitude to the master by transcending him."*

Max let that soak in, then continued: "Isn't that better-than-perfect thinking? You see the master as perfect, but he wants you to be even better. In the best relationships, both people are masters and both are disciples.

"So who was the teacher at my company? I don't know. All I know is that I wanted to inspire John, who'd come back with something wilder than my notion, and then we'd get ourselves in a spiral of inspiration.

"John and I both felt that to be ordinary, to just do something routine, would be a defeat. We had to do something special every time. The interesting thing is that we never talked about it—we never made it a stated goal. It was just *there,* in the room with us, as an understanding.

"It reminds me of the best sentence I've ever heard a businessman utter. The man was Peter Schutz, the former CEO of Porsche, who described a similar feeling about a colleague as:

"I like me best when I'm around you."

"That's what we're searching for—people who aren't just competent. We're not looking for people who make you love them or their work; we're looking for people who make *you* better, and make you glad for it.

"That's not in any job description I've ever seen, which means that you can't get there by working harder or smarter or even perfecting your job.

"We're looking for the people who make work special. These are better-than-perfect employees, and they are the jewels of their companies. And that's my goal for both of you, to be one of those jewels."

Angelina was moved and said, softly, "Wow." And even though we were meeting to talk about Angelina's career, not mine, I knew that we had an understanding there with us in the room: To be counted among the jewels was something we both wanted.

Part I

The Face of Creativity

or

"How Wonderful Could It Be?"

The suspense is terrible. I hope it will last.
　　　　　　　　　　　　　—Oscar Wilde

We'll jump off that bridge when we come to it.
　　　　　　　　　　　　　—Lester Pearson

———————————————

It turned out that our rendezvous would indeed be in Phoenix, which thrilled Angelina, who is always cold and who hoped for a heat wave in the desert. We arrived in the late afternoon—it was more than 90 degrees, and still early April—and were driven to the Royal Palms, an elegant resort at the base of Camelback Mountain. There we discovered that my uncle had chosen the "romance package" for Angelina and me. This meant that we had champagne and chocolates awaiting us in the room, and that as we ate dinner in the hotel's restaurant, dozens of candles would be lit around our room.

A note from Max told us he'd be meeting the next morning—*late* the next morning. What an uncle, that Max. In fact, as a kid, I thought 'great uncle' referred to a really terrific relative, like my Max. Even now, when I hear that expression, I think of him and smile.

Max made arrangements for a driver to pick us up the next morning and take us to meet him at the art museum on the campus of Arizona State University. Given the man who'd chosen the location, I almost expected some wild-looking structure, but instead found a chunky concrete building that looked to be a storage facility. Only as we entered, a level below ground, did I discover that it fit the desert, being a cross between a cave and a castle, and that the setting fit Max, for it was a series of surprises.

Max was in the lobby, wearing a baggy, seersucker suit with the usual bolo tie, entertaining the staff with some story. When he saw us, he concluded with them quickly; then, with one arm around me and one around Angelina, led us upstairs, charming Angelina as we walked.

The Jewels of the Collection

He took us to a gallery with a startling display spread across the wall of one large exhibit room. Instead of the usual horizontal row, this wall was covered with paintings of faces, each by a different artist, and each in a different style. And I mean *covered*—high and low, with just inches between frames. There must have been 30 or 40 of them—grinning, glaring, wise, silly, realistic, and fantastic. Instead of studying a painting at a time, this wall said, "Take a look at art looking at you."

Angelina topped my appraisal with her response: "It's the face of creativity."

If you know Max, then you know that he reacted with a gasp of delight and insisted on giving her a high five. He told us that he thought of meeting at a museum because every art collection had it's 'jewels.' Then he pointed out some of the paintings on the wall that he thought qualified and asked us to pick our favorites, then, being Max, turned it into a lesson by saying, "Why do you single out those particular pieces?"

Angelina replied, smiling and thoughtful, "Some make me smile and some make me think. And a few do both."

We all liked that one: smile and think. We all knew that we were getting close to the essence of better-than-perfect colleagues. Max asked Angelina, "Okay, now if you could take one painting home, which would it be?"

Eventually she chose one with stunning workmanship about which she said, "I could lose myself in that one. I could just stare at it and dream."

Max brought us around to the lesson, saying, "You, Angelina, have made our first point. Every good employee knows his or her job, just as every artist in here knew his or her craft. All are talented. Most use that talent to perfect their craft. Some, however, are better than perfect. They have something more than talent—they have style, which means they have uniqueness. And then the famous few, the great artists of all time, combine talent, style, and uniqueness into a story. They engage the imagination. They make you want to know more. Isn't that the allure of the most famous painting of all, the *Mona Lisa*? Michelangelo's genius was that you see her, and want to see more; you *want to know*. She engages the imagination. She pulls you into the story of what could be."

Max was wound up now, and a frowning security guard got him to lower his voice, although we were the only ones in the gallery.

He continued by saying, "A symphony orchestra is sometimes used as a metaphor for business, with an executive as the conductor. Well, the other night I saw an interview with one of my favorite conductors, Michael Tilson Thomas, music director of the San Francisco Symphony, who was talking about how he chooses the pieces to perform. He got excited talking about the moment of selection, saying that he has such regard for the brilliance of his musicians that he doesn't ask himself the boring work question, 'Can we pull it off?' No. Instead, he asks the question:

"How wonderful could it be?"

"That's the dreamer's question, the artist's query. And that's just what my best employees have done for me—just like my best bosses, clients, and suppliers have done, too—make my thoughts go up a size. They lift the eyes from the path ahead to the horizon. How wonderful could it be?"

Okay, I'll grant you that Max is given to overstatement. You could say that Max's life was an overstatement. But he certainly did engage the imagination. I said to him, "That's a good question to ask about Angelina's career. She has so much talent—I'm looking at her and thinking, 'How wonderful could she be?'"

We both stared at her, wondering. She rolled her eyes.

Max next led us to a conference room. He'd arranged to borrow it, and he'd brought along a bag of books and notes. Here was a guy who could have had a thousand briefcases from Rodeo Drive, and a staff of assistants to carry them, but he chose to lug around a paper bag instead.

He started us off by saying, "Okay, we each had our assignments. I trust they were completed." I saluted and Angelina nodded. "Then who wants to go first and tell us your best jewel-hunt story?"

My Jewels

Angelina turned to me, and I was glad to start. First, I should back up and tell you that the company I work for does development projects, including master-planned communities. And when we put in parks, the playground equipment comes from a company in Minnesota called Landscape Structures. Let me pick up the story as I told it to Max and Angelina:

"One of the employees at Landscape Structures was a guy named Norbert Stahlberg, who was a German citizen, living in the U.S., and working as a welder. Sadly, Norbert was killed in a motorcycle accident a few years back, his body flown to Germany for burial. Even now, all these years later, the people at the company still talk about him.

"He was just a welder—and I mean *just* in the sense that he was not a manager or even the most senior guy—but he was the leader of the manufacturing process. He was so good at what he did that everyone looked up to him and came to him for advice. He became the unofficial overseer of difficult questions. The way they talk about him, he was the Godfather of product quality. And here's the capper to the story..."

I paused a bit to let some suspense build. "He was so revered that people in this company have flown to Germany to visit his grave. Can you imagine? Some of these people are rural types who've never been out of Minnesota, but they fly overseas to pay respects to their fallen colleague."

They were impressed, and Angelina asked, "Did you learn anything about how he became that important to the culture of the company?"

"I wondered that. One HR consultant who works with Landscape Structures, Brian Gagan, told me that the German welder made you feel like you could accomplish anything. He put it, 'After talking to him, I felt that even I could weld.'"

Max was pleased with the example and repeated the part about him making you feel you could accomplish anything. Then he added, "You can see how such a feeling would spread as people would try something new and want to bring it to him. That's the specialness virus we talked about before. It spreads via curiosity. You can see how different that is, compared to just being the perfect welder."

Max stopped himself, not wanting to jump too far ahead. I, however, wasn't ready to stop. "Can I tell you another one?"

"Overachiever," said Angelina with mock sarcasm.

Meanwhile, Max merely grinned, so I jumped into another case study.

"This one is about a guy I'd love to work with. A friend told me about Chris Miller, a senior VP with Novastar, which is a mortgage company in Kansas City. So I called him, and he was very gracious with his time and wisdom. Here's a story that tells you what kind of guy he is.

"Miller is in charge of several departments. One day, he starts off by meeting the person responsible for recruiting new talent. Then, an hour later, he was in a meeting with the people in Collections, talking about losses from delinquent accounts. In that second meeting they had a discussion of the causes of good accounts going bad. Turns out that one of the leading causes of defaulting on mortgages is when people lose their jobs. And because Miller had just been thinking about hiring, he asked himself a wild question: Would the hiring of career counselors reduce the number of bad loans?

"So Miller puts numbers to the idea. A loan going into foreclosure ended up costing the company about a third of the principal amount. So a quarter-million dollar mortgage going bad would cost the company over $80K, each time."

Max couldn't wait for the rest of the story, "Please tell me they went ahead and tried it."

"Yes. In the first year, they counseled nearly a thousand people. The company spent $330K on the program while saving about $2.5 million.

"But what I liked best was hearing what it does for the employees of Novastar, especially in Collections. They get to tell themselves stories like the one they told me: One customer had been unemployed for six months after losing a job he'd had for 20 years. The career counselor quickly realized that the man hadn't interviewed for a job in more than 20 years, and was simply unprepared. Within 45 days, he had a new job, paying more than his old one."

Angelina sighed. "It would be terrific to work at a company open to that kind of thinking."

"Exactly. Miller was a carrier of the specialness virus. Listening to him, I wished I could work with him; I wanted to be in on the next revolutionary idea. It reminded me of your telling us, Max, about you and a best-ever colleague getting on a spiral of inspiration, feeling that to do something ordinary would be a failure. That was the energy that flowed from Chris Miller—what *else* could we try?"

Max felt my energy and then gave some back, saying enthusiastically, "Isn't that the essence of creativity? That is the way of the artist. Further, what you have demonstrated in those two examples is that you can find genius anywhere, at any level—you have given us a manufacturing firm and a service business, a welder, and a senior VP. Nicely done, my friend."

Angelina's Jewel

Angelina was eager to tell her story. She'd hinted to me that she had a hot one, but had insisted on my waiting to hear it.

"We have this terrific woman who does public relations," she began. "This woman, Raleigh Pinsky, qualifies as a company jewel, but I remember what you said on the phone, Mr. Elmore."

"Max," he insisted in a stage sigh.

"Okay, Max," she said shyly. "You said that you were going to contact people you admired and ask them about who makes them better, so that's what I did with Raleigh. And am I glad I did, because she told me about her better-than-perfect client, and it's somebody famous. She even said, with prompting, that they loved him so much that everyone in the PR firm did their best work for him."

She, too, was going in for some suspense building and it was all I could do not to yell, "Well, *who was it*?" Max saw my impatience and winked.

Angelina turned to Max and said, "Have you heard of the band Kiss?"

Max said, "Sure, but don't ask me to hum any of their tunes."

"Well, Raleigh's best-ever client was Gene Simmons of Kiss."

"He's the one with the tongue," I offered, before I realized how ridiculous it sounded.

"Raleigh was once with a PR company in Manhattan and he was one of their clients. She worked with him and Sting and a whole list of stars.

"It turns out that Gene Simmons was raised overseas, and when he came to this country he started out by working as an office temp. Raleigh said he was a 'Kelly Girl,' which is what they used to call them, I guess. He's a great typist and very proud of it."

She smiled, picturing what she was about to tell us, then said: "Every year, during the holiday season, he'd show up at their offices and would go around to each secretary and take over each one's job for a while. They'd all save up typing or filing and put him to work. And of course, everyone would take pictures of him at their desks and get him to autograph presents for friends."

She smiled to let us know she was finished, but then abruptly added, "And the other thing about him was that he was famous for calling and thanking them for their work. Every time they got him an interview, he'd call. You'd never know it to look at him, in character, but in dealing with the PR firm, he was one classy guy."

Max was making notes. "Okay, that fits nicely into our pattern."

"Good," responded Angelina, "because I keep thinking about it, but I'm not sure how it applies to me, since nobody would want my autograph."

Max wagged a finger at her with mock seriousness, "Don't try to get me to jump ahead, young lady. We'll bring it all together before the sun sets."

Max's Jewel

Max stood and bowed to me, then to Angelina, and repeated the line about transcending the master: "You have both come up with powerful, meaningful examples. I am indebted to you both."

I knew Max would have something just as good, and he did. He told us the unlikely success story of Steve Ray.

"As you know," Max began, "I've been asking everyone about this notion of people who raise the level of work of those around them. And I was meeting with a couple of TV guys—Mike McFadden and Joe Reynolds, who do corporate videos and network television stuff for Skyline Productions. In a lull in our meeting, I explained what I'm looking for and both said simultaneously, without hesitation, 'Steve Ray.'

"They explained that they're working on a series of videos for Ignatius Press, the Catholic publishing company, and Steve Ray is the narrator.

"But let me stop and back up a minute. Ray has an amazing story, leading up to the video series. He owns a building maintenance company in Michigan that he started with only a used Hoover that he bought for five bucks, and some homemade business cards. And by homemade, I don't mean those business cards you can get today and make on a computer—these were hand-printed on index cards he'd cut in half. From that start, he built a company of 500 employees, doing $12 million a year.

"Somewhere along the way he decided to become a Catholic. He wrote a book about his conversion, and that eventually led to this video series.

"So the two guys I'm working with are going on about how this Steve Ray lifts them up and gets terrific work from them and everyone else. So I say I'd like to meet him and it happened that he was coming to town to shoot some studio footage to wrap around the location scenes.

"I show up and watch him in action, and there was a telling moment: They shot some narration footage and when it was done, he immediately asked for suggestions. He was told that it was perfect. The director and crew are ready to move on and say so. That's when he says this simple but amazing thing. He asks:

"Do you think it could be better?"

"This stops them. They start to contemplate how it might be better. And Ray says, with obvious enthusiasm—I'd have to call it 'boyish' enthusiasm—'Let's try it!' And they shoot again and it *was* better. I was back in the control booth, watching the crew, and they were looking at each other and nodding, amazed at the improvement over the first take.

"What impressed me was that his question— Could it be better?'—was pure. He truly wanted to know their opinions; he wasn't trying to manipulate them. And here's what's important: He's a complete novice at that type of work, so he didn't know how to make the documentary any better; he just sensed when there was an opportunity to engage the imaginations of those who did."

This seemed to me to be an important and useful insight. I could see that simply asking, "Do you think it could be better?" could be a test of every project.

Both Angelina and I had plenty of questions of our own, which centered around, "Is that all it takes? Just asking a question?"

Max explained that when he met with Ray, he'd simply asked him a question that amounted to this: "I've heard you lift up whatever group you're a part of. How do you do it?"

Ray countered by saying he wasn't conscious of raising the level of people around him, but he did suggest that he had an ability to 'feel a situation.' In other words, he was aware of the feelings of those around him.

However, that merely took us to another question, which was, "How to have heightened awareness?" Max had thought about this, and gave us a remarkable example, quoting Steve Ray as saying:

> *"I believe that people aren't just molecules and hormones; we all possess infinite value and I have to treat everyone that way."*

Max said, "The way he emphasized the words *have* and *everyone* made me understand that he saw no other possibility. I *have* to treat *everyone* that way.

"When I got home that day I looked up a quote I'd saved from Nathaniel Brandon, the psychologist who specializes in self-esteem:

> *"What a great teacher, a great parent, a great psychotherapist, and a great coach have in common is a deep belief in the potential of the person with whom they are concerned. They relate to the person from their vision of his or her worth and value."*

"In other words, they don't just see the person, but the potential." With that, Max asked, "So, what do our three—no, four— jewels have in common?"

Angelina pulled a face and recounted the labels of each of the better-than-perfect colleagues: "There's a rock star, a mortgage VP, a welder, and a narrator/entrepreneur. They all made our list by being examples of best-ever colleagues: one as a client, one as a factory leader, one as an innovator, and one as a teammate on a production crew."

"But what made them best-ever material? How do they do it?" Max insisted.

I took a shot, saying, "It's like our discussion of great paintings—they don't just demonstrate their talent, they change how you feel. With great colleagues, they change how you feel about yourself and your work; they make you want to live up to...." I wasn't sure of the word—was it *example* or *standard* or something else—then it hit me: "Maybe I should just stop there—they make you live *up*."

Max gave me one of his awed looks and then wrote it down.

"How wonderful could it be?" Angelina added, solemnly. "Imagine how it would be if you lived your life with 'how wonderful could it be?' as your guide."

The Sammy Davis Jr. Effect

After a bit more conversation, Max declared it was time for lunch—after all, we hadn't gotten started till nearly eleven o'clock—and we set out across the campus, eventually ending up at the University Club, one of the oldest buildings on campus, which had been converted into a restaurant.

As we ate, something Max said brought back a dusty old memory. Here's what he said to prompt it:

"One of the people I talked with about best-ever colleagues was Barry Brooks, who, along with his wife, owns Cookies From Home. He told me about one employee who was especially valuable because she was his opposite. Along the way he described her in memorable fashion:

"She loved to work and loved the work."

That little sentence has come back to me many times as I've talked about admirable people," Max told us.

That's the story that called to a deep memory of mine. I said to Max, "Way back, when I was a teenager, you took me and my sister along with you to Las Vegas. Do you remember?"

Max's eyes went northeast in contemplation. "Yes, it's coming back. Didn't we get kicked out of a casino?"

"Absolutely. You were letting me play the nickel slots and some beefy security guys came up. You tried to convince them your arms had gone numb and I was merely acting on your behalf. You twisted your body so your arms flopped around. That's when they grabbed us and walked us out."

"I hope you weren't too emotionally scarred. No gambling addiction? No fear of neon lights?"

"No, I suppressed the whole misadventure. But something important happened later that day. You dragged me to see a Sammy Davis Jr. concert. I was against it, but you insisted. And something transpired that I wouldn't have believed: I loved watching him. A scrawny guy singing songs I detested. Still, I loved the show.

"I loved watching him because he *so* loved what he was doing. After one of his songs, he announced that he'd had an idea of how to do the song better. He asked our permission to do it over, and had a chat with the bandleader, and they did it again. Maybe that was a gimmick, but I didn't care—I was with him. What won me over was watching someone who enjoyed his work that much. *That* was the show."

Angelina added a marvelous thought: "You see someone who isn't just for-hire, but who is deeply involved with the work, and it's spiritual, somehow. Do you know what I mean?" We both did.

During lunch, Max pumped us for what else we'd learned doing our jewel-hunt. He took notes, nodded a lot, and when he'd gotten all we had, told us to walk around the campus and to meet him back at the museum conference room in an hour. He was heading straight back and wanted to integrate our findings into his.

"When you arrive," he promised, "I will explain just what it takes to be the sort of colleague who makes everyone better, a better-than-perfect colleague. Our goal will be to possess their genius, and the result will be that everyone you work with will consider you *the* person they want on their team. You are going to be first-pick for the most important projects at your company."

Angelina winced. "That's a lot to ask."

"Nope," replied Max merrily. "As one of the Zen masters explained, if your heart is set on the goal of realization, 'you are already a baby Buddha.' Our hearts are set on our goal, are they not? Then we are baby jewels, ready to sparkle with the spirit of exploration."

Part II

How Better-than-Perfect Colleagues Think Differently

or

In Praise of Lovably Unreasonable People

Until you know that life is interesting—and find it so—you haven't found your soul.
                              —Archibishop Geoffrey Fisher

Here is my lesson from the heavy rain: On your way, you meet a shower. You dislike to get wet, so you hurry along the streets, running under the eaves. Still, you get wet all the same. As long as you accept that you will get wet, you won't suffer from being wet.
                              —Tsunetomo Yamamoto

———————————

Angelina and I strolled the campus, feeling that unique college energy, the special vibration of minds being stretched. Then we took our time seeing the rest of the art museum, but couldn't make ourselves linger any longer and headed back early to the conference room.

Max had spread dozens of index cards around the conference table. They were in columns and stacks, some white, others pink or blue. They seemed to be in advancing columns and thus brought to mind a toy-soldier battlefield scene.

I suppose you could say that it was a scene of Max doing battle with the forces of mediocrity. And watching him work, bouncing on his toes, humming and muttering, anyone could see that he was one of the intelligentsia of business, one of the jewels.

"Sit," he commanded. "The stars are aligned and we have our answers. There are three of them." He slapped the table in three places. "And I have selected the most intriguing one to start with. I'm calling the first facet 'In Praise of Lovably Unreasonable People.'"

He paused to let us register surprise and puzzlement—although we knew that, with Max, any answer would raise new questions—then he jumped in, loving the work, loving to work, and with an audience that was grateful to be a part of it.

Max held out his hands and made a broad stripe in the air, indicating one of his sections of the table. "Each of these cards represents a case study, and we'll get to several of them, but let's start by examining the ones we've already discussed.

"First, there's the marvelous story of the rock star—what was his name again, Angelina?"

"Gene Simmons."

"Here's the question: Was his going into the offices of the PR firm and doing their work a logical thing to do?"

Angelina looked as though she wanted to argue the question, but said, "It was sweet."

I jumped in, saying, "I think I see where you're going. The logical thing to do would be to just send flowers or a fruit basket. And in economic terms, where you try to maximize utility, he could have made tens or hundreds of thousands of dollars by spending that day doing a concert instead."

Max pointed at me, agreeing. "That's what I want you to understand, that old Mr. Logic is setting traps for us—snaring us in ordinariness. Starting a business with $5 of capital and homemade business cards is not a reasonable way to start a business. Flying across the Atlantic to visit the grave of a former co-worker does not fit our known patterns of logical behavior.

"Let's back up and look at where logic would get us if we were advisors to a rock star and talking about what to do for his business associates for the holidays. How would we do it? We'd ask ourselves or friends, 'What do other people do?' And we'd hear that they send a poinsettia plant or whatever. And we would do the same.

"And if he was a big star and he said, 'I should do something special,' then we'd tell him to shell out for the really big flower arrangement. That's the normal way to do it. It's reasonable—you *reason* your way to the solution. That's how you try to be the perfect client. That's not what we have here. What we're talking about are unreasonable acts."

Angelina made a little frown and I could see she was debating whether or not to interrupt. I gave Max a look and inclined my head toward her and he immediately understood and asked her, "What do you think?"

"But it *was* logical and reasonable, at least in hindsight. They all did their best work for him, so it was worth his time or his economic utility or whatever you want to label it."

After considering for a moment, Max said, "Good point," and clearly meant it. "I think the key word in what you say is *hindsight*. Here's the problem: When we ask our brains to come up with a solution, it begins a search of the mental encyclopedia of ideas, looking for a workable solution among all the known solutions. *Known* solutions. And that's what's important here—logic takes us down the path of the familiar.

"If we ask other people for ideas, we just get them to travel their paths of the familiar. So, the issue is how do we jump to ideas that are brilliant in hindsight but don't typically appear along the road taken?"

"I see what you mean," Angelina said. "It demands a different level of logic, a leaping logic, rather than the traditional thinking."

Max laughed at the image of leaping logic, but Angelina was determined to come up with a name. "It could be 'hyper-logic' or 'trans-logic,'" she offered.

Max pointed at her, nodding and declaring, "I like trans-logic. We get to the unreasonable by going across the logical. But hyper-logic sounds better—I don't know, it sounds high-tech. Let's agree on that one," Max declared. "And see if we can figure out how to build a hyper-logic device. We'll do it for clients or customers, for employees, for managers, and for entrepreneurs or businesses."

The Lovably Unreasonable Customer

"As you know," Max continued, "I called people I admire to ask them about admirable people, and one of the first people I thought of was an old friend and genius, Davis Masten. I know he has some terrific people working for him, so I expected to hear about employees who challenge him—and he had some, as expected—but what I did not expect was for him to wax on about one of his *customers.*

"Davis heads Cheskin+Masten, experts on packaging. So he's the guru, although he's gone beyond 'guru' to the higher plane of 'woowoo.'"

Max looked at me and said, "When I start to digress, just say 'Your point?' Okay? Try it."

"Your point?"

"Exactly. It's to tell you about how a customer who is relentlessly trying to find better ways to do his or her job inspires you to bring her *your best work.*

"Davis started by telling me that because his company has more work than it can handle, they choose their projects based on whether the client is worthy of their talents. He put it more diplomatically, but that was the essence.

"He recounted for me a meeting they'd had the day before, when he told his staff that they'd been asked by a research manager of a major corporation to submit a proposal. He asked the group of 18 people, 'Who's worked with these folks before?' Twelve hands went up. 'Okay, who wants to work with them on this project?' No hands. And that was it—they declined to bid on the job."

"Your point?" I asked, smiling.

"Ah, the point. To seek people and projects worthy of your best work. If you do projects just to get them over with, you'll never grow and never be worthy of great clients.

"Which brings us to the point, which is tell you about this particular client of Davis's, Lynda Firey-Oldroyd, an executive in San Francisco. She's now taken a new job, but Davis had an example from when she was at Levi's—you know, the jeans company.

"Davis began his story about Lynda by saying, 'We are cocky about how innovative we are and so we love a chance to show off. That's why we love clients who throw the hardest questions at us. For instance, when Lynda was at Levi's, she had been part of a big customer segmentation project.'"

Max stopped to see if we were following him. Angelina assured him by saying, "We did segmentation at our company. Instead of trying to sell to everybody, the company came up with five customer types, and we focus on two of them."

"I don't know how it worked out where you are," Max said to Angelina, "but in my experience, most market research has little effect on how the company does business. In the case of Lynda Firey-Oldroyd and Levi's, the company had spent big money on defining these types of customers, but it hadn't had much effect on the company's designers. As Davis put it, 'The trick isn't spotting trends, it's making that knowledge part of the culture of the organization.'

"'She pushed us by asking us a new question—how to make the information more useful to the designers. She was, in effect, asking us—an information company—how to turn information into wisdom. Great question, right?'

"I wish you'd been with me when I talked with Davis, to feel his joy at remembering being taunted by that question. And so, instead of just trying to understand how to sell jeans to customers, they had to understand how to sell ideas to designers."

"So how did it work?" Angelina asked.

"I put that question to Lynda. She explained that she was a marketing person who'd had the sudden realization that her group was doing a lousy job of marketing their data to the company executives, doing the usual research reports and PowerPoint presentations. The irony was that they were selling the idea that different types of customers thought differently and yet hadn't allowed for the fact that the company executives, designers, and merchants had different ways of thinking, too. So she got Davis and his team to offer results in several ways."

Max counted off the three ways:

1. The team brought the various customer segments to life by finding customers who embodied each segment, and having them attend the presentation of the findings.

2. The team made an interactic CD-ROM with pictures of the various customer

types, including photographs of their lives that the team got from giving customers free cameras and getting them to take pictures of their everyday activities.

3. They created cards summarizing each type, which then went on a chain with a belt-hook, so the designers could literally wear the information.

"Said another way, they didn't just do a perfect piece of research, they went well beyond mere research, all the way to wisdom, and thus became better than perfect."

Max grinned and said, "That's more than you wanted to know about that project, I'm sure. But I wanted you to see how wonderful hyper-logic can be. The typical corporate person would have just shrugged and blamed her co-workers for being numbskulls and not 'getting it.' Instead, she went to some bright people and got their eyes glittering with curiosity. Which just happens to be our key word for the day: *curiosity*."

Angelina responded immediately: "She got to hyper-logic by rejecting the currently available options. She started with the assumption that she needed something original."

"And that's why she called Davis. I asked her if she threw tough questions at all her suppliers, and she told me:

> *"Whether it's suppliers, employees, or internal customers, I try to know three things about them—their expertise, comfort zone, and passion. Knowing those, then I can stretch them, without asking too much and paralyzing them."*

"Which means," I suggested, "that she would know just how unreasonable to be with each person. That's the 'comfort zone' part. But if she paid attention to their passions, then she'd know how to—how did you put it, Max—get their eyes glittering?"

"Exactly," Max responded. "And it turns out that one of the facets of our company jewels is a hyper-awareness of their colleagues, but that's getting ahead. Let's stay with 'Lovably Unreasonable People' just a tad bit longer."

"Good," said Angelina immediately. "Because walking around the campus made me think of a story about an architect."

Max, eyes glittering, turned to her and said, "Omit no detail."

The Old Lady and the Architect

"A guy I grew up with went on to become a professional musician," Angelina told us. "He plays for the Los Angeles Philharmonic, and when I was in Los Angeles on business last month, he took me on a tour of their new building, Disney Hall. You've probably seen pictures—it's all curvy metal walls. Unbelievable."

Max slapped the table. "I've *been*. It's stunning. Literally. You first see it and you just stop, frozen in amazement. And I have a story for later about the man who hired the same architect, Frank Gehry, to do the now famous Guggenheim Museum in Bilbao, Spain."

Angelina continued: "Then you probably know that the hall was a tribute to Walt Disney, with much of the money coming from Lillian Disney, his widow."

"But that's all I know about it. Tell me more," said Max, rolling his hand to encourage her.

"The story that you hear about the building is that Mrs. Disney gave the architect pictures of brick buildings covered in ivy and suggested the concert hall have that same look. But instead of looking like something in a Thomas Kincaid painting, the Hall is this ultramodern, curving, metal structure. So the conclusion is that the old lady got duped. But that's just wrong. In fact, I met one of the people on the project team, and he said there was a move to dump Gehry as the architect, and Mrs. Disney insisted he stay, threatening to withdraw her money if he was replaced.

"What *really* happened is this. Gehry didn't dismiss Mrs. Disney's photos; he studied them. He went to Lillian Disney to discuss why they appealed to her. And they understood together that she wanted the 'feel' of those buildings. No, not even that. They agreed on *how they wanted visitors to feel* when approaching the hall.

"And then later, he sent her a bowl of white roses, her favorite flower. And he told her, 'It's going to look like this.' And the building does resemble a flower. And it was going to be white, and stone, till Gehry was talked into changing it. And inside the carpet and seats are a floral a pattern that Gehry designed and named 'Lillian.' The building isn't at all like those sterile modern ones—Disney Hall embraces you, calls you to come inside. Just like a brick cottage with ivy and flowerbeds.

"And one last thing. This is so sweet—Gehry went to visit Mrs. Disney at her house, and she showed him her collection of Royal Delft porcelain. You know the stuff, it's blue and white, from Holland?"

She looked at us to see if we knew what she meant and though we didn't, we both urged her to continue.

"He created a fountain to go in the courtyard of Disney Hall that is a giant rose, covered in pieces of broken Royal Delft porcelain. You could miss it if you didn't go up a level from the street." Max shrugged to indicate that he hadn't seen it.

"The story about the photos," Angelina said, with conviction, "makes it seem like he went around her, or tricked her, but I think she charmed him and he charmed her and they ended up inspiring one another. What do you think?"

Max grinned at her. "Thank you for that story. I went to a concert at Disney Hall, and I was lucky to get a ticket. They were sold out every night. All because Lillian Disney and Frank Gehry got themselves in a spiral of inspiration, starting with a fascinating question: How do we want our visitors to *feel*? Ask a great question and see if something wonderful happens. And the building is hyper-logic brought to life. The building doesn't make sense, but there it is, welcoming you."

"Oh boy," Max moaned, "look at the time. We have to pick up the pace. I think we have some solid clues here about how to be a client/customer that everyone wants to work with, and who gets the best work out of people. We need to work up from feelings to make sure colleagues are both appreciated and stretched. Done right, *we show our appreciation by stretching them.*

"When you say, 'This is a tough problem and I need a brilliant solution,' that's a grand compliment to the right person. You are offering him or her a chance to be a hero.

"That's a gift. You offer a unique gift and you get one back. That's the new logic of the best-ever customer—give the most and get the most. Agreed?"

We both nodded. "Good, because we have much more unreasonableness to cover, as a manager and as a business. But first, the trickiest one of all, as an employee. Are you up to it?"

The Cunningly Unreasonable Employee

Max insisted that we stand up and stretch, telling us that the next example was his favorite. "This involves a woman who reminds me of you, Angelina. She works for a giant computer supplier, Avnet. Her name is Lisa Boudreau. The other main character in this tale is Rick Hamada, a charismatic executive who heads the division where Lisa works. These are both people I've gotten to know and so I was there to watch this one happen.

"Out of a group called The Innovators' Lab, Rick and his team had come up with an idea, to create a new type of customer service person, what they called the 'Avnet Concierge.'

"The idea was inspired by the service at the Ritz-Carlton Hotels, how the employees don't point you to where you're trying to go—they escort you. At Avnet, when customers called their sales reps, they sometimes asked questions the reps couldn't answer and didn't even know who could—after all, this is a $10 billion company—with lots of different product groups. So the rep would transfer you and then maybe you'd get transferred again. The idea of the Concierge was that the reps had someone to escort you, via phone, and make certain you got helped. And the rep would stay on the line and learn from one of these super-reps they were going to call the 'Concierge.'

"Rick chose one of his star employees to make the program happen, the Director of Customer Satisfaction—that's our heroine, Lisa. There's a stunning amount of information these new super-reps needed to know, and Lisa was to find the prototype person and create a system that would make customers purr with satisfaction. A massive job, but she dug into it.

"I called her one day, to see how it was going. She said, 'Well, I was going to hire a new person to be the prototype, then I found out we have a hiring freeze. Plus, we haven't gotten back all the information we need to support all the groups involved. Plus...' She added item upon item and my spirits sank, sorry to see the program die. But then she said something miraculous. She said:

> *"But we're starting it anyway. We'll begin next month. If we can prove it's worthwhile, maybe we'll get the resources."*

Max stared at us, making sure we were impressed. "You see what was happening here. She didn't have the budget, the people, or the information. It wasn't 'the right time' and she wouldn't be able to 'do it right.' But what she understood was that it's never 'the right time' and that you never have everything you need to make certain you're going to 'do it right.' So she ignored the reasonable thing—to postpone—and figured out a way to start a test project.

"And guess what happened next?"

"Well," said Angelina, "you wouldn't be telling us the story if it didn't succeed, right?"

"Right. But it's *how* it succeeded that's critical. Her boss, Rick Hamada, was so impressed by her courage and determination that he figured out how to get her the budget she needed, after all. In other words, she took things out of logical order. She didn't go one, two, three—she went one, three, two. Not a logical order. Not reasonable. Just brilliant. It isn't always 'find the resources and then get started'; sometimes it's 'start, and the resources will find you.'"

Angelina gave a small gasp of revelation, telling us, "Given the way it happened, her boss probably could *not* have told her to go ahead and start. That would be too much to ask. So she freed him from the snare of reason."

"Ah! You have surpassed me once again. Yes, while the best bosses stretch their employees' talents and skills, it's one of the traits of the best-ever employee to be self-stretching, and even to stretch the boss."

The Bigger Job—Circles of Helping

Max nodded to me and said, "I believe you had a good case study on that point." I knew exactly which one he meant.

"Right. I ran into my insurance agent, Mary Contreras, at the bookstore, and I asked her about colleagues who lifted her up. She got this gentle look on her face, that one-week-into-a-two-week-vacation look." I was proud of that line, so I paused a beat to let them picture it, and they both got it—that look, I mean. Here's how she described her best-ever employee:

"'I was a young woman when I was put in charge of a department for Sperry. These were engineers and technical people, almost all older than I was. I'd had a former boss and mentor, Clarence Johnson, who'd retired, and I managed to persuade him to come back and work in my department, part-time. And not too long after he joined me, there came a day that changed me.

"'I was assigned to do a big presentation to a tough audience. These were people who could give the company a big contract, and they were skeptical of anyone young, much less young *and* female. A few days before I was to do the presentation, my old mentor—now employee—asked me if I was prepared. I told him 'absolutely,' trying to be self-assured. Clarence just shook his head and said, 'No, you aren't.'

"'I insisted that I was, and he said that was fine, but suggested that I rehearse the presentation for him. He was right about my preparation because he asked questions that revealed all sorts of holes. So together we did role-playing, thinking through all the people who'd be there. He had me create a notebook on every contingency.

"'I went to the meeting. I walked into a room full of skeptical engineers, and walked out with the contract. Clarence was my ally, coach, mentor, consultant, and employee, all at once. I'd always been a shoot-from-the-hip type, and he taught me what preparation is.'"

Max complimented me, then started with his questions, all of which came down to: "What can we learn?"

Angelina made the connection to the theme of the hour: "It took courage to hire her old boss—after all, she was trying to establish herself as manager, and hiring him could have been seen as weakness. And the employees might have gone to him instead of her. So she had guts. And he did, too, of course. To go back in at a lower level, reporting to an old employee. I think if either of them had asked enough people for advice, they would have each been talked out of it. They would have heard, 'Be reasonable' and given in to the fears."

"And," I added, "that this is a roundabout instance of 'how wonderful could it be?' starting with, 'how awful could it be?' He showed her the weaknesses of her presentation and her style."

"Well said," Max replied. "He was watching her back, which wasn't in his job description, so he went well beyond perfect. But he surely understood, having been in her position, that hollow enthusiasm is worse than useless; it's dangerous. It amazes me how many employees relish the possibility of seeing their boss fail. Maybe they're hoping he'll get the ax and they'll get his job. But that never happens. If the manager fails, the entire department is tainted. Upper management will want someone from outside to turn things around."

"That doesn't seem right," Angelina insisted.

"At some level executives know that great employees are part of circles of helping, while mediocre ones stand on the side of the pool, leaning against the life preserver and looking the other way. Or, at the very least, executives realize that great employees are not going to work for a lousy boss and will find ways to change departments or companies. So if your boss stinks, and you just stand by, it's hard to get the smell out of your clothes."

"Speaking of bosses," Max said, "it's time we take a peek at them. First, though, can we agree that if you're going to be a best-ever employee, you're going to take it upon yourself to be a do-it-anyway person, and you take it upon yourself to raise the level of everyone around you. Your job isn't your assignment—your job is creating circles of helping within the organization. So you help your boss get a new contract. And you help your boss start a new program even though the budget isn't there. So you become the world's most valuable welder, not by your welding, but by setting a standard of quality and style for everyone on the factory floor."

Max grinned at his own enthusiasm. "Let us praise the unreasonable employee. Can I get an 'amen'?"

We gladly obliged.

The Lovably Unreasonable Boss

"Nobody ever says they want an unreasonable boss," Max began, "although the best bosses—the ones I like to think of as gifted bosses—realize that they have to get to hyper-logic. They understand what George Bernard Shaw meant when he said:

> *"Nothing was ever accomplished by a reasonable man."*

Or when Tsunetomo Yamamoto, the author of *Bushido, The Way of the Samurai*, wrote in the 1700s:

> *"Sane men, of calmly composed mind, cannot accomplish a great enterprise."*

"I have another example," I offered eagerly, fighting the urge to raise my hand and wave it.

"I took a tour of the Gallery Furniture in Houston. It's the largest single-location retail store in the country. They have a policy: 'Buy it today, get it today.' They have *same-day* delivery—of everything.

"I asked the owner, Jim McInvale, how they did it, and he said, 'Well, a lot of times we put the furniture in the truck and follow the customers home.' But then he showed us the warehouse, and everything is built for flow—the furniture comes in the big doors at the back and right out the docks in the front. They built the place around that unreasonable promise of getting it to you the very same day."

Max grinned and indicating me with his head, said to Angelina, "I just love this guy."

"Me too," she told Max, then turned to me: "But I don't know if I'd want McInvale as a boss, given how driven he is."

"It's part of being shrewdly illogical. What's the logical thing to do when you have a successful retail outlet? You expand to other locations. But not Gallery Furniture! Another thing you do if you're successful is build yourself a great office. Not McInvale. He doesn't have an office. He stands at the front counter all day long. That way, he says, he can spot any customers who are leaving unhappy and intercept them before they leave having had a bad experience.

"The whole place is weird in an appealing way—there's a tennis practice court inside the store, a tribute to Princess Diana and Elvis. Free food. Live bands on weekends. That kind of thing."

"He turned the store into an adventure for customers, right?" Max asked, and I nodded. "Is an adventure an encounter with the expected or the unexpected?"

We all nodded at the obvious answer.

The Workplace Adventure

"The best bosses know how to make the workplace into an adventure for their employees," Max told us. "The man who heads research and development for Fender guitars, Dale Curtis, created what he called the Frog Works, a play on the old notion of the Skunk Works.

"But he didn't just imitate other corporate labs; he chose as his role model the lab run by the character 'Q' in the James Bond movies. He created a playful environment and got upper management to agree to let him insulate his group from the corporate world of logic and deadlines. His group has no conventional plans, schedules, or reporting. Nothing reasonable about that.

"And the group has just one goal, to come up with new products that make musicians say to one another, 'Have you seen it yet?' They started with how they want customers to react—just like Frank Gehry sitting around with Lillian Disney."

———

Max looked at his watch again and, comically accelerating his rate of speaking, said, "I have to throw in one final example, because it adds a dimension of calling to the imagination. This one is from a company called Fort Dearborn. They're an international packaging firm and I got to attend their 'final four,' which is what they call the finals of their innovation competition. There were actually five teams invited to the finals, but that's how it goes with hyper-logic executives.

"The Fort Dearborn competition was centered around President Rich Adler's theme of 'velocity,' which in manufacturing means reducing lead times and cycle times and inventory. The employees of Fort Dearborn responded with 26 entries in the competition, ideas that saved the company more than $5 million that year.

"Although most of the innovations were around technical issues that went over my head, the company reinvented its selling, in part by figuring out how to efficiently do mock-ups that will allow customers and prospects to see how their product would look in the latest packaging.

"Rich Adler, the president of Fort Dearborn, even built innovations into the budgets. This sounds cruel, to budget in improvements that don't exist, but if you'd been there at 'the finals' you would have seen that it was just the opposite. It enlivened work, gave it a sense of risk and exploring the unknown—and that's a pretty good definition of adventure."

Angelina gave that high-wattage smile of hers and added, "We're back to redefining the give-and-take of employment. Part of that is redefining the concept of giving. A challenge is a gift. A tough assignment is a gift. It's like offering someone a trip; a journey to someplace new."

That got Max applauding and he even threw in a "huzzah!" Then he suggested that we talk while strolling out to the courtyard of the museum.

Max stopped next to a sculpture and took a moment to appreciate the beauty of the stone carving. Then he continued, "There's one *other* way a manager can be lovably unreasonable."

The Mitas Touch

"This example is from Dr. Connie Mariano, who is also *Admiral* Mariano. She was the president's doctor, on the staff at the White House, for the end of the first Bush term, then for Bill Clinton, and also for the start of Bush the Younger.

"And I have a great story to tell you later about her wisdom on choosing and running a staff, but for now I want to tell you about her boss, prior to her appointment at the White House.

"Her boss was Dr. John Mitas, who headed the medical staff at the Naval Hospital in San Diego. One day Mitas called Connie into his office and said that he'd been reading the requirements for White House doctor, and that he was thinking of nominating her.

"Her ambitions had never taken her imagination down that path and, taken aback, all she could say in reply was 'I'm not so sure.' He said, 'Well, I'm sure you could do it. I'm nominating you.'

"He did, and she won the job. She traveled the world with three presidents. And there's a sweet postscript to that story." Max then digressed a bit, but I think it's worth repeating here, for it put the idea of being 'unreasonable' into context.

"Connie's father was a Filipino steward, and the U.S. Navy has a tradition of Filipino stewards working for admirals, doing their cooking and cleaning, and running general houshold errands. These stewards often enter through the back of the admiral's house, and sometimes bring their children along to work with them, all entering through the back door.

"And one of those children, Connie Mariano, became the Navy's first admiral of Filipino descent. In a ceremony in the State Dining Room, under a portrait of Abraham Lincoln, she was sworn in by President Clinton as the First Lady looked on. She chose her father to attach one of the golden shoulder-boards of admiralty. She says his hands shook with emotion.

"Can you see it in your mind? Can you feel how he must have felt? No coming in the back door that day; he came in the main entrance of the White House, and left as an admiral's father.

"Isn't that the beauty of this country? Isn't that the true American Dream? It's not materialism—it's the freedom to write your life story on fresh, clean paper.

"This country was founded by people who wouldn't listen to reason and work things out and stay in Europe, who wouldn't be patient and compromise with the English King. This country was founded by the sort of people who dumped tea in the harbor, the same sort of people who later set out in wagons and traveled west. This country was founded by the very people who wouldn't listen to reason." He leaned in and said, "In other words, we are living in the the 'Land of Unreasonable People.'"

Max smiled, knowing he'd gone further than he meant to. "I almost forgot," he added, quietly: "That day when Dr. Mariano got those golden shoulder-boards, someone else was there— her old boss, John Mitas. She says that he has helped so many people go on to exceptional careers that his former employees joke that they were given the Mitas Touch.

"Giving up your star employees is not conventional logic—it takes wondrous courage. And that courage takes us back to the people who not only can see beyond their own self-interest, but those who look at their colleagues and straight through to their best selves. You see what could be."

Max looked at Angelina and said, "What are you thinking?"

"That it's beautiful and I wish I were like that, but…" She gave a sad smile. "That's a leap. Like the hyper-logic." Her look said that she felt it was as far removed from her own life as jumping in a Conestoga wagon and heading into the wilderness.

Max gave her a kind look in return and reached out and took her hand. "You react that way because you have a wonderful old virtue called humility. Very much out of fashion. But it's one of the virtues you need to become one of those who is better than perfect. The other virtues are compassion, kindness, and dignity. I have it on good authority," he tilted his head toward me, "that you have those in buckets. The rest can be learned."

She made a face and said, "I think I may be stuck in the mode of being logical. I'm not sure I'm built for leaping."

"No, no," Max responded adamantly. "The hardest part is simply remembering to leap.

School teaches you to grind out assignments by thinking the way everyone else thinks. There's nothing you can do about that mindset now, so go with that flow. Find the logical solution and then—here's the magic—you go just a bit further. Don't stop when you have a good plan; instead, congratulate yourself on that good plan and then set it aside and ask yourself, 'How wonderful could it be?' Make it your reward for having found a solid plan—it got you to the place where you have a chance to leap. Are you with me?"

"Grind, then leap," she said, not sounding convinced.

"Yes! Only one person in a hundred gets beyond grinding, so it will feel different—it *is* different! And that's how you get to be special, by taking a shot at being different, every chance you get."

I thought I understood and added, "You look at people and see what they could be. You look at projects the same way. You see through what exists, and past the next logical step. You train yourself to see another dimension: potential."

Max applauded and said, "You have picked us up and leapt into the next topic."

Part III

How Better-than-Perfect Colleagues Learn Differently

or

The Sexy Brain

The dumber people think you are, the more surprised they are going to be when you kill them.

—William Clayton

Intelligence recognizes what has happened. Genius recognizes what will happen.

—John Ciardi

_____

Max led us out of the museum and up some steps into a courtyard where the museum joined a performance hall. An oboe player was sitting on the steps practicing, taking advantage of the accoustics of the high walls surrounding the courtyard.

We bought sodas from a vendor with a cart and sat on a picnic table while sparrows perched in the trees around us.

Max eyed them and began speaking: "Those birds remind me of something I learned recently. I was reading some research about crows, and how they learn from one another. And I stumbled upon an odd assertion that fascinated me: Crows can count, but only to six."

I knew I was supposed to say "Your point?" but hesitated.

Max read me—he always does—and said, "You're thinking, 'So? Big deal.' I understand. But there's a lesson there. If six hunters go into the woods and five leave, the crow knows one hunter is still in the woods. However, if seven go in and six leave, the crow thinks the woods are clear. To him, a bunch of hunters went in and a bunch came out, so all's well.

"You see the monstrous implications of this? Not just for the crow, I mean, but for us."

We did not.

Max grinned. "The crow thinks he's safe. He thinks he's on top of things. He can't see the danger because he doesn't know he can only count to six. He doesn't know that seven exists. The same is true for us: We don't know what we don't know.

"I once did a study of lousy bosses. Turns out, the less they know, the more they think they know. The worse the boss, the higher the self-appraisal. I once heard someone refer to the worst management as a 'cranial-rectal inversion.' In an odd paradox, when it comes to management, the bigger the head, the more easily it slips into the—well, the inversion.

"While doing the work on lousy bosses, I came across the work of Justin Kruger and David Dunning in the *Journal of Personality and Social Psychology*. They won me over as a reader, right from the top, because they opened with the story of McArthur Wheeler, a man who robbed two banks in Pittsburgh. In both cases, he made no attempt at disguise, he simply walked in for a simple stick-up. When the police nabbed him, they told him that he'd been identified from surveillance videos shown on the evening news. The guy was stunned and repeated, 'But I wore the juice!' You see, he believed that applying lemon juice made his face invisible to video cameras.

"In writing about that example, the authors quote Darwin:

> *"Ignorance more frequently begets confidence than does knowledge."*

"And then Kruger and Dunning get to their own research finding. They did experiments that tested each person's humor, grammar, and logic. In each case, those research participants with the *least* knowledge/skill were the *least able to judge their own performance on the tests*. I remember the statistics: The test scores of what they *actually knew* put them in 12th percentile, but when asked to rate themselves, they *estimated themselves* to be in the 62nd percentile.

"It turns out that as you learn a subject or develop a skill, you realize how much there is to learn. In fact, the highest-level performers scored themselves lower than their actual test results. It's the humility of the knowledgeable. Being wise isn't being vain—it's gaining appreciation, which is a form of humility. And that's why the best people have more questions than answers, and why they have networked brains."

Be My Watson

We wandered back into the museum, taking a new route, through a gallery of photographs of elderly people, the black-and-white photos bringing out their creases and wrinkles. Max made a gesture, taking in all of them, and said, "I wonder how many of these folks got wiser instead of just older. You hear old people moaning about how our society doesn't respect the elderly, but how many of them earned the right to be looked up to? Most of the old people I meet think that the meaning of life is knowing that Tuesday is Senior Discount Day at the cafeteria."

"Your point?" I said, grinning.

Max punched my arm, then thanked me, and explained that he had started having some of his business meetings in museums, an idea inspired by Sherlock Holmes, who would go to the art museum to try to solve a case, knowing that an image in a painting or sculpture, or a passing face or bit of conversation overheard, could spark a connection.

There was a point to the Holmes business. When Angelina and I arrived back at the conference room, Max pulled out a book he'd brought with him, Kristin Thompson's *Wooster Proposes, Jeeves Disposes*.

He began by reading a passage where she quoted from a detective novel by A.A. Milne— yes, the same man who created Winnie the Pooh—and Max had Angelina read aloud a passage where the amateur detective recruits a friend to help him:

> *"Are you prepared to be the complete Watson?" he asked.*
> *"Watson?"*
> *"Do-you-follow-me-Watson; that one. Are you prepared to have quite obvious things explained to you, to ask futile questions, to give me chances of scoring off you, to make brilliant discoveries of your own two or three days after I have made them myself and all that kind of thing? Because it helps."*

Max also had with him the Milne novel and had marked a series of passages with little colored stick-on flags, each passage an instance where the hero needed his friend to be, as he Milne puts it, 'Watsonish.'

It was interesting, but I was secretly a bit put off by the Watson example. It smacked a bit of the patronizing old business about how important the cleaning lady is to the NASA launch. Not something I'd expect Max to find helpful. I should have known better, for Max then had Angelina read a passage from one of Wodehouse's Bertie and Jeeves stories. Now it was Jeeves, the employee, who has all the solutions, and who bails Bertie out of so many difficulties that Bertie's friends come to Jeeves for help. When one of Bertie's stuffier acquaintances objects to involving "the domestic staff" in his problem, Bertie rebukes him by saying this:

> *"No, one does not want to keep valets out of this," I said firmly. "Not when they're Jeeves. If you didn't live all the year round in this rural morgue, you'd know that Jeeves isn't so much a valet as a Mayfair consultant. The highest in the land bring their problems to him. I shouldn't wonder if they didn't give him jeweled snuff-boxes."*

Max explained that his curiosity about great colleagues had led him to study the relationships of great fictional pairs. One of the notions he'd found in Thompson's book was that the relationships were 'marital.' There is a familiarity between the characters that has both creative and comic potential, but more important is the commitment to one another, despite their differences. If opposites attract, it is *not* the result of some perverse sense of humor in Mother Nature; rather, it's the completing of one another.

As Max put it, "With the first pair, it's Watson who stimulates Sherlock with his questions and Watson who gets to be around a genius; with the second pair, it's Bertie who stimulates Jeeves with his dilemmas. The position is lucrative for Jeeves, as he's routinely offered substantial rewards for his genius, but Jeeves also gets another, overriding reward: He gets to be a hero. Bertie and his friends are an appreciative audience for Jeeves's talent. Combine that with the intimacy of rescuer and rescued, and you have a marriage of talents."

I must tell you that most of this conversation had been going over my head, but there was something about that last bit, "the intimacy of rescuer and rescued" that made me reconsider.

Max jumped to the next point: "Said another way, it doesn't matter who's smarter, or who has the best insights into people, as long as you work together you have your two brains networked together, which is to say that you have a joint intelligence—a big, merged brain."

Angelina understood, for she said, "You don't need to know everything, just know who does."

And I got it too, and added, "If you know who knows, then *you* know. It's no different than having the answer in a book on your shelf or in a filing cabinet. It's *your* knowledge."

Max gave us a look of amazement. "Well, I guess you two have that principle wrapped in foil and stored in the freezer. Good. Now we can skip ahead."

Cerebra, Scrota, Cardia

"Remember the president's doctor I told you about, Connie Mariano?" Max asked. "Well, when she worked at the White House, she had to build a staff. And Connie was smart enough to know what she didn't know—and I don't just mean in specialized medical expertise. For instance, when it was time to hire someone who could train to be her replacement, she picked Dr. Richard Tubb. He did, in fact, replace her.

"Tubb had impressive credentials, but then again, all the candidates did. Connie once gave him a compliment that we all should aspire to, saying,

> *"The organization got better the day he came."*

"When I asked her what she meant by that, she said that he 'always closed the loop'—meaning that he knew how to communicate well. But she also said that he 'balanced her.' Working in the White House, she and her colleagues would talk about 'picking Cabinets.' They got to see that when you choose your advisors, you choose how decisions get made.

> "At some level, choosing your advisors is like answering questions before they're asked."

Watching several presidents work had made Connie realize, she told me, that you need 'a joker, a doomsayer, an analyst, and a strategist.' And then she confided in me that she'd once put it in medical terms, and reduced the decision process to three words, which she made into a screen-saver: 'Cerebra, Scrota, Cardia.' Or, brains, heart, and..." Max checked with Angelina, not certain how proper she was going to be.

"Balls," she said, completing the troika, making Max chuckle at his own reserve.

"The good doctor told me," Max continued, "that she was always bit too *gutsy*—always eager to jump in, and that's one reason she wanted Tubb on her team, because he was more cerebral, more analytical. My point is that if you are aware of your limitations, you grow your brain in that direction. You have to be aware of your limitations in order to think of ways around them."

"Add a lobe," I volunteered helpfully.

"Exactly. Okay, you get the point, so I won't go into other examples. But I want to make clear to you that when I asked people about better-than-perfect colleagues, I almost always heard some version of those same counterbalancing skills that Connie used. Which means that if you want to be a star, you have to work at being different, rather than working at conforming."

"You reminded me of that British expression for lay-offs," Angelina commented. "'Made redundant.' If you're redundant, you're surplus."

"Or," I added, "as William Wrigley once put it:

> *"When two men in business always agree, one of them is unnecessary."*

Max grinned and said, "So we can conclude that you have to keep adding new lobes to your collective brain. Which we could make into a marvelous life-enhancing goal: to add a new brain every week or month. It would force you to get out and explore other groups in and out of the department."

"I'll do it. Weekly," Angelina said, and I knew it would be easy for her, because she had a smile that would open doors, open bank vaults, even. Then I realized that I had it easy too, because I met a lot of people in my sales work. I only needed to establish a brain connection, which just came down to curiosity.

Brain Throbs

"We've all heard of 'heart throbs,'" Max said. "Or, wait a minute—*have we*? It's an old expression, come to think of it."

We assured him that we knew the expression.

"Okay, then let's talk about becoming brain throbs. You want to create a giant brain, but then make that big, gray guy work smoothly. You want people to think about you, think for you, and think with you. *We want them to be so delighted to hear from you that their brains throb with joy.*" Triumphantly, Max added, "In other words, you have a brain that's attractive to brains—a sexy brain."

I chuckled at the image and his enthusiasm but then shrugged and said, "Didn't we already cover that, with 'In Praise of Lovably Unreasonable People' and 'Trying to Leap'?"

"Precisely, my young friend. Now we're going to figure out just how it's done. Sometimes it happens just by stumbling upon an idea. Take your story about the mortgage company VP. What was his name again?"

"Chris Miller of Novastar," I told him.

"Your Chris Miller got your brain throbbing, just by telling you about his idea to hire career counselors. But look again at how he came up with the idea: He happened to have meetings with Recruiting and Collections on the same morning. He brought together two ways of thinking that usually don't go together, so his own brain got stretched.

"That's one way to be creative—to force together ideas that normally don't go together— and that's what most brainstorming sessions consist of. That's how you can get your own brain throbbing, and done right, it starts other brains throbbing.

"But now I want to talk about how to grow a merged brain, to get others thinking in such a way that they get to be heroes. It's time for another of my favorite examples, this one from a better-than-perfect executive at Blockbuster, the movie rental folks."

Questions Are the Answer

"One of their executives, Mike Roemer, the COO, had much impressed me. For one thing, he wanted to improve the stores, and he was smart enough to know he needed to find out what he didn't know. He knew he wanted store personnel to use their time wisely, but wondered, just how *did* they use their time? So he hired people to go into stores and watch. Just watch. The result was a list of 969 observations. Many of them amounted to the fact that 'customer service' folks spent very little time serving customers—36 percent of their time, to be exact.

"So Roemer recruited a number of bright store personnel to help analyze where their time was being diverted from customers. Notice that he created a big brain. And the upshot was to find dozens of ways to save time. They found they were able to reduce total hours worked, while increasing the time spent helping customers from 36 percent to 50 percent and climbing. Employees got to spend more time doing what they love doing—talking about movies—and so customers got more help, and overall costs dropped. That's the power of knowing what you don't know and embracing it. That's huge—like being the crow that counts past six.

"But all of that is just to say that Roemer was an impressive guy. And so he was on my list to ask about better-than-perfect colleagues. And he had a zinger for me, a rising corporate star named Shane Evangelist—a great name for someone skilled at bringing others along. However, he doesn't win people over by converting them, but by letting them convert him. *That's* a sexy brain."

(I stopped Max there because I was getting confused, and maybe you are too. Mike Roemer is the COO and Shane Evangelist is a rising star who reports to Roemer.)

Back to Max's description:

"When I talked with Mike Roemer, he immediately began telling me about Shane, who recently turned 30, but is already being put in charge of significant projects for Blockbuster.

"'Why?' I asked Mike, and he told me this: 'He reeks of leadership. He energizes a room. He used to be a gymnast, and in one meeting, in his business suit, he jumped up and did a 360 degree flip, just to shake people up. And then he's great one on one, too. One time he was flying with an employee, and Shane got upgraded to first class, being a frequent flyer. But after take-off, he went to an empty seat in the coach section, next to the young employee, and spent the entire two hour flight talking about that employee's future."

Max gave us the inquiring eye and Angelina obliged by saying, "There's the idea of leaping beyond the expected—literally, in the first case."

"If you want people to sing your praises, you have to give them some lyrics." Max stopped and grinned. "Oh, that one was *good*. Hold on, I've got to write that down.

He did, and then continued. "I was curious about energizing a room in two minutes, so I followed up on how Shane does it when he isn't doing flips. Mike said:

> *"He doesn't try to offer solutions, he*
> *just reminds everyone of big goals.*
> *He paints the picture."*

"When I then asked how he paints the picture, Mike told me I should ask Shane. So I did. First off, I wasn't surprised when I told Shane I'd been hearing how terrific he was from Mike Roemer, he said, 'Whatever positive things Mike said about me, I could tell you double about him. He's the best.'

"Then I got to the point and asked him how he 'paints a picture' and gets people to see big goals. He philosophized a bit, but then gave me an example of how it works in practice."

Max winked at me and said, "Take notes." But I was ahead of him there, already writing.

"Shane was put in charge of starting the Internet version of Blockbuster, where the movies get mailed back and forth. He knew that the profitability of the venture depended on the efficiency of filling the order—of taking the customer's request off the computer and getting the DVD in the mail. He'd learned that if the employee could complete an order in 60 seconds that would be acceptable. So he went to his team and said: 'I'm wondering if there's some way to get the transaction down to, say, 50 seconds.'

"He explained: 'I didn't know how to get it to 50 seconds, all I was trying to do was paint the picture that efficiency was worth studying and working on. Then the team came back and said they had gotten it down to 40 seconds. So we got to celebrate and build our confidence that we were going to beat expectations.' And that," Max concluded, "is how questions are the answer. Be my Watson and stretch me, or be my Jeeves and astound me. I don't care if you're the employee or manager, questions are the answer."

Beaming at us triumphantly, Max said, "Great example of a sexy brain, no?"

We had to agree that it was, especially since it gave me a breakthrough in my own thinking. I'd been having trouble envisioning how I was going to get from identifying new lobes to recruiting them into a big brain—and, even more troublesome—how I was going to get to the point of being 'lovably unreasonable' with them. Now I understood. I didn't have to have the answers, just plenty of "what if?" and "what else?" questions—that was how sexy brains called to one another.

Being in sales, I knew a lot about asking questions to try to get customers to reach the conclusion that they should buy from me. The purchase is much more likely to stick if their minds come to the conclusion that my plan is the best, rather than my forcing the conclusion onto their minds. Now, however, I saw that this was different. My old line of questioning was trying to guide them along a map, whereas this new route was heading straight off the map. The picture I could paint was that there was something better out there, a better way to work together, and we'd help each other get there.

Angelina had an example of her own. "I have a brain throb to tell you about," she began.

"She's Marie Casey, out of St. Louis. She's one of the jewels. Because of the way she is with people, her communications company is busy. And Marie got frustrated because she had this new side business, involving corporate histories, that she just couldn't find time to work on.

"Exasperated, she complained of that frustration to a consultant who was trying to help her organize her life. To Marie, it was an impossible problem because she wanted to make her life simpler, not add another new business. The consultant said:

"Why not ask your employees for help?"

So Marie decided to do just that. And her employees were delighted to help her. They told her to work at home one day a week and they'd cover for her. And now she's starting the new project and loving it."

Max started to respond, but Angelina quickly said, "Wait! I have one more thing. Marie told me that having the consultant ask questions like 'Is that decision in alignment with what you want from life?' has prompted her to start asking her staff tough questions. Every month she has a meeting and asks her employees, 'What have you learned?' Isn't that a scary-great question to know you're going to be asked every month?"

"Scary-great is right," I answered. "But it would fit in with growing a big sexy brain."

"Absolutely," Max agreed. "And I want to talk to this consultant. Can you get her name?"

"Sure. I met her. She's Jan Torrisi-Mokwa. I have her card at home."

Speaking of tough questions, Max then recounted for us his conversation with a pair of screenwriters, Leo Benvenuti and Steve Rudnick, who have done several films, including one I'd enjoyed, *Kicking and Screaming* (the comedy with Will Ferrell and Robert Duvall as soccer coaches). Max was keen on what he called the Hollywood model, which he defined as thinking in terms of 'gigs' that bring together talent to take on a specific task. Also, he wanted Angelina and me to think in terms of 'takes.' Here's how Max put it:

"When I asked the screenwriting duo about their role during the shooting of the movie, they were energized by their recollections of working with the director, Jesse Dylan—who happens to be Bob Dylan's son. They lit up, talking about what they called a '*true* collaboration.' 'What was that like?' I asked them. Dylan got them to feel truly involved by getting them to give him something beyond their best work. After all, they had worked hard to produce the best possible screenplay—they had turned in their best work. However, after getting each scene down on film, Dylan would invariably say some version of, 'Okay, we got that. Anything else?' Or he would just ask, 'Anything else you'd like to try?' As Benvenuti put it, 'It looks different when you're shooting. You find strength in one of the actors and go with it. Or you throw out an idea and let Will riff.'"

Max reached out and grabbed my shoulder, "Does that sound familiar?" I told him it did, that it was like the guy doing the documentary series and the "grind, then leap" conversation we'd had.

"Bingo. You get one take 'right' and, instead of stopping, you use 'right' as the starting point for creativity. Getting the first version down doesn't lock you in; it frees you up. 'We know we have something good to use, now what else can we try?'

"Imagine working for a guy like Jesse Dylan—where you truly feel involved because you know you're going to get asked 'what else can we try?' You can't ever think your work is perfect, because you're always going to get a shot at making it better than perfect. And so your mind is alive with possibility."

We then began to discuss how we could get colleagues to be 'alive with possibility' when we worked together.

That led to an example of particular interest to me, as it gave me a revelation about a higher-order version of selling. Max had met an executive from a company that works with cell sites—the towers for cell phone transmissions— obtaining the land and zoning and all the rest. Here's what Max told us:

"I was working on our jewel-hunt on the plane. And, of course, I ask the guy next to me if he has any thoughts. His name was Bill Mara, and he told me how his company had gone from just doing site acquisition, to doing management of sites, a much bigger business.

"They heard that one of the giant wireless companies was looking to hire a property management firm to take over the sites. The founder of the company, L.G. Lyle, said, 'Can we bid?' Innocent little question, the kind you get to ask if you're out there talking with customers. The answer was yes, and they did.

"But the plot thickens.

"There was a second round of bidding and our little Lyle Company was not invited back for the second round. Meanwhile, however, Lyle had pulled together a group of vendors, clients, and insiders to discuss how the industry would change over the coming years. So instead of just feeling sorry for themselves, they kept learning.

"Then, while the second round of bidding dragged on, the folks at the big wireless company let them take over a few of the sites—temporarily, just filling in till one of the big property management companies was selected. Eventually, there was a third round of bidding, and the folks at Lyle were invited back in, and they now had more specific industry and client knowledge than any of the big guys and—bingo—they got the giant contract."

As I said, that story was validating, because I had already realized that, as a salesperson, I had a chance to ask customers a lot of questions, usually as a way to get them to learn about my offerings. But as this example illustrates, when you and the customer *learn together*, you take them on a journey to a place where your competitors vanish—curiosity is *the* competitive advantage. And that took us to a discussion of how to put curiosity into action.

Experiments Never Fail

One of Max's aphorisms comes back to me often, almost daily: *Experiments never fail.* By that, he means that, if you're experimenting, you've got a shot at an improvement and, even if things don't work out as you hoped and you go back to what you were doing before, you go back a different person, having gotten practice at breaking the status quo. Moreover, whatever idea it is that you're playing with, you're boosting your brain allure—after all, you're playing with ideas, not just planning or evaluating or meeting about them.

The notion that 'experiments never fail' fits nicely with Max's story of the woman who started the Concierge project—she didn't have the resources to do it right, but she went ahead anyway. I suppose you could argue that it was actually better to start as an experiment, rather than to labor under the glare of a big-deal new initiative.

Since the day we met with Max, I got to spend some time at NASA, as part of a benchmarking project for our industry association.

One of the most impressive people I met there was a soft-spoken genius named Steven Gonzalez. I got him talking about better-than-perfect colleagues at NASA, and he told me of several, including two I want to tell you about, both of whom found ways to speed up work via experimenting.

First, he spoke of a 'lovably unreasonable boss,' the sort who nicknamed his team the Pirates and reveled in loud arguments about projects and who also reveled in getting things done in months that used to take years.

Steven told me that the speed came from finding the shortest route to, "Let's see if it works." For instance, in redesigning the lay-out of Mission Control:

> *"It wasn't proposals and committees, it was bringing in consoles and moving them around until we had a design."*

The result was that everyone wanted to work for him. It's amazing how an anti-bureaucrat can attract talent—the best people understand that experiments never fail and want to be part of that play-around, see-what-happens energy.

Steven also spoke of another colleague, Tony Bruins, who created something they call 'the virtual human.' This is a computer program that predicts where astronauts will have problems in space. Steven said, "When you build anything to go into space—a suit or a vehicle—you have to see if it's ergonomically suitable. For instance, it might not occur to you that, in space, a place of major strain is the top of the foot, because you have constraints there to keep you from floating off. We always started with the human body and built around it. Now, however, we start with a model of a human. The 'virtual human' shows where pain occurs, such as 'pinch-points' in suits."

That success with the 'virtual human' inspired Steven to suggest to Tony that he develop a lab for investigating new technologies. Tony jumped into that project, despite having no budget, and pulled together a team of corporate and university talent, and the new lab was soon thriving.

This is another case where not having a budget at the start was liberating, because with budgets come proposals and reports and committees—I picture trying to run a mile with a couple of accountants hanging off your back. But Tony got started, and then the money ran to catch up with his energy and enthusiasm.

By the way, when Steven spoke of Tony, his eyes lit up and he gave him this marvelous compliment:

> *"He's infectious. He has the ability to pass on the vision, to give everyone their piece, to let everyone find their place in his passion."*

If you're like me, you want to have that effect on people. But I'm getting ahead of our story.

Great to Good

The next example came from an article Max pulled out of his paper sack, and it came from the Website *www.ChristianityToday.com*. Where Max finds this stuff, I can't tell you, although he has told me that his curiosity is contagious, and people think of him when they read interesting articles, so he has a lot of lobes in his connected brain.

The article was called 'Great to Good Churches' by Eric Swanson. If you're like me, you read the first part of the title as being like the book, *Good to Great*, but this ran the other direction.

Swanson wrote, "Many churches are seeking to become great churches. Entire ministry industries exist to help that process—from fund-raising, to church building programs, to worship resources, to programming. And in nearly every community there's at least one great church, as measured by numbers and facilities. But large churches discover a troubling secret. Size alone isn't good enough."

Swanson argues that the urge to be great can distract from the immediate ability to do good. He says, "Maybe from God's perspective, the greatest thing we can do has more to do with goodness than greatness." And, "With the overwhelming problems that people have, we often think, What good will this little act of kindness do?"

What it can do is illustrated in Swanson's recounting of a church in Pasadena that held a Super Bowl party for the homeless. What good could that do? About 250 people had a good time one afternoon. Big deal. And yet that's just what it became—a big deal. The party evolved into a weekly dinner and Bible study, and now the church is planning to build transitional housing apartments. Swanson says of these small, starter programs, "Not every church can go from good to great in the traditional sense, but perhaps it is in going around doing good that we become great—no matter what our size."

As Max and Angelina and I discussed the great-to-good, we saw how perfectly it fit our conversation. I suspect it's true in churches, and it's certainly true in the corporations where we worked: Individuals are rarely handed the resources to do it right, or rarely asked to design something great and go out and make it happen. No, what most management amounts to is "work hard, do what you're told, and don't screw up." That's the old 'be perfect' management thinking. Yet each of us has the chance to make things better by asking, "How can we make this a little better for our customers?" The accidental result is to make things better for us, too. You accept that things aren't great but steal moments of greatness anyway. That's how you move to better-than-perfect thinking.

Starters and Closers

Max was telling us of another strategy to better use your larger brain. "Let's talk about a man I admire, Dan Sullivan, who heads the Strategic Coach, a company that works with successful entrepreneurs. He came up with what he labeled the '80 Percent Approach.'

"The idea is that you undertake a project, but instead of completing it, your goal is to get it 80 percent of the way to complete. Then you hand it off to someone else, who takes it 80 percent of the remaining distance. You keep going until you get as far as you need to go.

"Sullivan argues that you get a better result, faster. He gave an example, from his own work. He likes to do his own graphic design for the company's materials. He says it takes him most of a week to get a design finished. But then he tried an experiment. He got it 80 percent of the way. It took him two days, I think it was. Then he passed it off, and in another day, it was finished, and better than he could have done it himself."

Beaming, Max asked, "The three of us are in a position to know why, right?"

Angelina spoke first. "He tapped into the bigger brain."

"And," I added, "he was able to jump into the project, without the pressure of having to know how he was going to make it perfect. It was great to good and back to great again."

"Yes. And I want you to know I'm not just passing along a theory; I tried it. I was working with some executives to develop some new retail ideas. We broke into five groups, and each one worked on a different theme for the new business. Each group put their suggestions onto a piece of poster board and presented it to the group. Then, I went around and took each poster board and passed it to the next group, and told them all to spend a few minutes trying to improve on what was on the poster board they'd just been handed.

"They started slow—I even had people saying, 'Oh, it's *perfect* the way it is.' I urged them to reject that idea, explaining that 'perfect' was a trap that stopped thinking." Max stopped there to make his hands into an old-fashioned bear trap.

"You see how that would happen? As soon as someone says 'perfect,' then the brains shut down. The word *perfect* is the off switch for creativity." Max was pleased with that one and waited for us to agree. I did so gladly, for I was truly catching on to the idea of 'better than perfect'—the person who rejected perfection and sought something still better would always go on alone, accepting the honor of being the pioneer.

But our mentor was moving on, explaining his experiment with the five groups: "So I pushed them, and *voila*—the level of ideas soared. I would say it doubled the creativity, and in 15 minutes. Everyone there was stunned to see what popped out on a second try.

"And then I asked them what they thought would have happened if each group had stuck with their original plan for an extra 15 minutes. They agreed that the improvement would have been slight, maybe 5 or 10 percent. Instead, the creative output doubled.

"People don't want to turn loose of their ideas. In fact, they tend to keep them quiet, not wanting to lose credit for them, I suppose. But I want us to agree that we can't hang onto them, that as soon as they seem to be something like 80 percent complete, we have to ask others to jump in. Let's assume we've missed something. The right people will love to be asked for their help. It's brain throb stuff."

The Sexy Brain Mating Call

Max then gave us a couple of instances where wise leaders had managed to create what amounted to brain-attraction devices. The first of the examples was that of Winzeler Gear, headed by John Winzeler, who decided that he didn't want to be competing on cost alone, cranking out bids to supply gears for projects ready to go into production. Rather, he wanted his company to be part of the complete process, including design. When he built an addition to his factory—it's in an industrial area near O'Hare Airport—he included an atrium art gallery. It was designed to attract designers—he wanted to offer his offices as a place to meet to work on innovations. His cool meeting space was his ticket to be in on the earliest stages of product design and to change himself from just a low-cost supplier into a brain throb.

The other example was of a company that used low price to issue its idea mating call. Max heard about them from Alvaro Gallegos, the inventor of Z-CoiLs, those shoes with the big spring under the heel. Gallegos had been toying with his idea for years, and then one day he got a mailing from a man named Yong Oh Lee, offering to make any sample shoe for $50. Gallegos bought samples, and Lee's company became the manufacturer of Z-CoiLs. The $50 price was ridiculously low—*unreasonably low*—but that was okay. The point wasn't to make money on samples, but to be the first choice for making samples, and thus be in on the ground floor for the development of new shoes.

"By the way, as I recall that instance, it was a little crazy of Gallegos to think that he could create a better shoe than Nike or Reebok, with their armies of designers, engineers, and technicians. But then he met Yong Oh Lee, a man crazy enough to want to lose money on creating samples. So we have two lovably unreasonable people finding one another.

"With John Winzeler and Yong Oh Lee, we see two men who became brain throbs by jumping to hyper-logic and refusing to accept the shrinking role and shrinking profit margins of being a typical supplier."

The Art of Being Criticizable

Rising to pace while he talked, Max said, "Let's try something. Let's walk around the table while we talk. See what happens." I felt a bit foolish to be circling the big conference table, but it felt good to be moving; after all, we'd been in the same room for most of the afternoon by then.

"During that last discussion," Max said, strolling, "we got very near an important topic, one that we should discuss before we close this section. And it's a tidy coincidence that Angelina brought up Disney Hall and Frank Gehry."

Tearing Up Genius

"I heard a speech by the man who hired Gehry to build the museum in Bilbao, Spain, and who hired him again to build the new

Guggenheim in Manhattan. That man would be Thomas Krens, the director for all the Guggenheims. Someone in the audience asked him why he went back to Gehry. His answer fascinated me:

"You can criticize him."

That was all he said, and moved on. But later I arranged to meet with Krens, and right away, I followed up on that comment. Was he saying that Gehry had no ego? No, he insisted. In fact, he said:

> *"Gehry has a bigger ego than any architect I know. He knows he's a genius. But he knows that he's so good, that if he does it over, it will be even better."*

"Krens contrasted that to most architects, who want to debate every point. With Gehry, he explained, 'If you don't like it, he's happy to tear it up.'

"Happy to tear it up. Can you imagine? One of the reasons why he feels that way is that Gehry is an experimenter, a just-start-and-see what-happens sort of worker. He does extremely crude drawings, then paper models. Krens sat with me, imitating Gehry, curving pieces of paper and sticking them to the table with Scotch tape. In fact, Krens did an appealing Gehry-esque design in a minute.

"Imagine how far you could get if you could play with dozens or hundreds of designs, instead of having to focus in on one or two to construct regular models."

As usual, Max gave us one of his isn't-that-wonderful looks. Angelina hesitated. She said, "I know this is the practical application session, and so I'm trying to think how to apply that one to my work. Nothing's coming."

"Okay. First, there is happily tearing up your work. The art of being criticizable includes having the self-confidence that the next time will be even better. Then, it's a wisdom that takes us back to experimenting and adding lobes, which takes us to the next strategy."

Romancing the Brain

"I know a few executives," Max said, "who always ask for multiple solutions to any problem. But you, as an employee, don't need to wait to be asked. Come in with three un-asked-for solutions. It's how professional creatives, like those at ad agencies, work. They know the idea they like best is rarely the same one the client likes best.

"Besides, as we discussed early on, the brain goes first to old ideas and, if still pushed, then it next constructs logical new plans. You have to push beyond that to get to hyper-logic. Just remember: The first solution is borrowed. The second solution is logical. The third solution is genius."

Angelina beamed as she moved gracefully around the table. "I have just the place to try it. My boss gave me a project, and I have a solid solution, but I'll give him a couple of others. Before today, I'd always given him a solution that I knew he'd like right off. I'd even ask myself, 'If *he* were doing it, what would *he* do?' Now I realize that I was *thwarting* the notion of the bigger brain by trying to make my brain overlap his, which is really impossible. I was just doing the job the same way he would have done it. So this time I'll give him the expected one, but I'll add at least one that will scare him—and see where we end up."

Max reversed his circular strolling so he could give Angelina a high five as he circled back past her. Max said, "Brava! Just remember that when you give him the alternatives, he may not be receptive. That's fine. Resist the temptation to think he's a dullard or a bureaucrat. After all, he's probably stuck in the status quo just like almost everybody else. The important thing is that you keep growing the brain.

"Never let your mind be divided. Never forget that you are working *together*, but, as it says in the samurai guide *Bushido*:

> *"No spirit and no talent is necessary so long as you have the ambition to shoulder the whole clan by yourself, to carry the burden alone if necessary."*

Angelina opened her mouth but nothing came out. Seeing her confusion, I jumped in to match it with my own: "But I thought we were working on cooperation here, not working alone. What happened to the sexy brain and multiple lobes?"

Max nodded. "Right. The point of the *Bushido* is that you are aligned in pursuit of the good of the clan—in this case, the organization and its customers. Once you are, then criticism is pure. Criticism is *welcome* when your only goal is making improvements for the customer, and that happens when you are willing to 'shoulder the whole clan.' Let me back up and deal with the issue I skipped, which was how to get alignment, to raise any criticism above the personal and into a mutual improvement."

Turning to Angelina, he said, "I happen to have a magic way to get alignment. If you want to increase the odds of your boss embracing the scary idea, you have to ask him questions instead of declaring your brilliance. Here's my favorite alignment question:

> *"Do you think this might help our customers?"*

There's magic in those words, because you've gone from merely tossing out an idea—which means risk and work for you *and your boss*—to inviting him to work together for the good of your customer. And that includes internal customers. Make sense?"

"Yep," she replied with a grin. "Instead of him thinking, 'Is Angelina worth this trouble?' he'd be thinking, 'Is our customer worth this trouble?' Most of the time, the answer to the former would be no and the latter would be yes." She apparently didn't care for the sound of that, so she added, laughing at herself, "But he *likes* me."

Max squeezed her shoulder. "How could he not? But if he didn't, the 'would it help our customers?' question would work even better because you're taking yourself out of the equation."

"And what," I asked, "do you do when your boss wants nothing to do with ideas and tells you to just shut up and do your job?"

He gave me an exasperated look and with mock sharpness said, "Hey, I thought you were in sales. What happens if you trick or bully someone into buying from you?"

"That's a hand-grenade sale—you run and it blows up. In other words, they back out and never buy from you again."

"So what do you do instead?"

"I get them to see how it's in their self-interest."

"And what if it isn't, in their eyes, in their self-interest?"

"I try another approach. Or, if it truly isn't in their interest, I walk away—my head up and their door open when I have a better plan."

Max pretended to be perplexed. "So what was your question about selling ideas, again?"

"Never mind."

"Wait till you hear the example I'll give you in the next session. A billion-dollar sale, by a non-salesman."

Part IV

How Better-than-Perfect Colleagues Communicate Differently

or

Growing an Organizational Third Eye

What you can't communicate runs your life.
                                        —Robert Anthony

We're in such a hurry that most of the time we never get a chance to talk. The result is a kind of endless day-to-day shallowness, a monotony that leaves a person wondering years later where all the time went.
                                        —Robert Persig

———————————————

Once I was done, Max decided that he'd had enough of the museum and he gathered up his bag of research and his rows of cards, showing us that only the row he called the 'Organizational Third Eye' remained. "These," he said, "we can cover at dinner. How do you feel about some Mexican food, *muy caliente?*"

Angelina surprised me by showing enthusiasm for the idea. Max had charmed her—not only her mind, but apparently her palate, as well.

After time at the hotel for lounging and checking messages, we got in Max's rental car and set out. He'd chosen a Toyota Matrix because "it was the most unusual looking car they had" and we went driving across the valley toward South Mountain. We headed down Central Avenue, past the restaurant that was our destination, so Max could see South Mountain Park, which he informed us is the largest municipal park in the country. I could see why—it was a desert mountain range, not calling for a lot of upkeep. We drove through canyons at twilight, the saguaros standing guard, and we fell silent in awe of the empty majesty of the place.

There was nothing silent about the restaurant, however, an energetic place called Los Dos Molinos. The salsa was fiery and the margaritas icy, so our mouths were soon merrily confused.

From Just-In-Case to Just-In-Time

"Okay, let's get into this last section," Max suggested, getting out his little stack of index cards. "Here's a little story that will get us into our topic. It's from Dan Hagerman, who runs operations for a company that sells bakery supplies to—well, I guess that's obvious, isn't it? He has a warehouse and a lot of trucks and drivers to be responsible for. He told me that he used to say to his employees whenever he left the office, 'If you need anything, don't hesitate to call.' And they called his cell phone all the time, letting him make every decision. And Dan, being a very *aware* type of guy, realized that the relationship had become one where he was the 'dad.' And if he wanted his staff to grow to self-sufficiency, it was up to him. So he made a simple alteration in what he said to them: Instead of saying *'If you need anything, don't hesitate to call,'* he'd say *'If something comes up that you can't handle, call me.'* His calls fell by 90 percent."

That example surprised me, but not as much as another one Max tossed out. He described an experiment reported by Bob Cialdini, the country's leading social psychologist, done by a restaurant that wanted to reduce its no-show rate on dinner reservations. The management tried changing what they had employees say to callers making reservations. Instead of saying to them, *'Please call if you have to change your plans,'* they instead asked, *'Would you please call if you have to change your plans?'* That was it—they added two words.

Max said of that experiment, "It wasn't the two words as much as going from a *statement* to a *question.* Guess what happened to the no-show rate?" He took a drink of margarita to force us to think about it, then said, triumphantly, "If fell by more than 60 percent! Can you see the significance of that?"

I could, although I was glad he didn't ask me to explain it. Instead, he carried on: "Dan Hagerman cut his calls by 90 percent. The restaurant cuts no-shows by more than 60 percent. Both by simple changes. Why so powerful? Because they established expectations for the information exchange. Further, the restaurant example had another lesson—getting people to commit by asking a question instead of issuing a directive, showing us once again the grandeur of the question mark."

We did the fire and ice treatment for a while, each of us contemplating the grandeur of the question mark, then Max tapped the table and gave a little speech that I thought was especially important.

"Everyone tells you that communication in an organization is critical—blah, blah, blah. The result is more and more communication—pronouncements and updates and memos and reports and e-mails—so much that it makes people less well informed. That's why one of the traits of the better-than-perfect colleague is that he or she delivers information when and how the receiver needs it.

"You know how manufacturing is J.I.T.—Just In Time. One executive I met—he was head of Harley-Davidson at the time—says their company had so much excess inventory at every stage of production that they were J.I.C.—or Just In Case. Most organizational communication is J.I.C., while the best-ever colleagues are J.I.T. They have developed a corporate third eye, one that lets them know exactly what others need to know, up and down and alongside them in the organization."

Max then shifted to specifics, letting us know how to deliver the right information at the right time. "Let me tell you about Steve Hardison, who has to be the highest paid executive coach in the country. Listen to this: He charges $1,500 an hour. And you can't just buy a few hours. You sign up for two-hour sessions, every week, for 50 weeks. Paid in advance. Do the math."

We did. Yikes!

"He believes that the commitment is a major contributor to its effectiveness, and talked of a study of cancer patients who travel to clinics, and there's this correlation: The farther you travel, the longer you live. But you're letting me get off the point. What do you get for all that coaching money? Communication at a level you've never experienced. Hardison says he's trained himself to hear what isn't said. What *isn't* said. He calls it 'the mortar between the bricks.'"

"But Max," I objected. "You're talking about a 'corporate third eye' and 'hearing what isn't said.' I thought this was going to be one of the practical sessions."

Max did a stage sigh and said, "It takes some building up to. We have to build up the momentum to *leap*."

The Organizational Third Eye

Max turned practical by referring back to one of the people we'd talked about earlier, the young star of the Blockbuster company, Shane Evangelist. Max said, "When I talked to Shane, I asked him how he energized a room. He said he felt he knew how to 'read a room' but that he didn't know how he did it, that it was innate. But as we talked on, he realized he *did* know how he did it, it had just become second nature.

"For example, take that incident his boss told me about, when he did the flip. He thought that was spontaneous, after reading the room. However, he went into that meeting having studied everyone who'd be there and he knew that he was going to get resistance and he needed some way to change the atmosphere. He studied for the test—the right test. Most people get ready for a meeting by rehearsing what they are going to say—which is fine—but it's studying for the quiz not the final exam."

Tapping my shoulder with his index finger, he said to me, "Let's put it together. This is as practical as it gets."

I grinned. "Thank you, Dr. Third Eye."

I thought he might have been annoyed with my crack, for Max stared at me with a frowning expression, unlike him, until he explained, "I'm trying to wink at you with my third eye." Then he started back in: "Shane told me that before every meeting he thinks through everyone who will be there and asks himself, *'Who needs to be recognized?'* and *'What does each one need, at a motivational level?'* In other words, it isn't about him impressing people; it's about honoring and helping people. Which is pretty impressive. Now, think back where we heard that kind of talk earlier."

Angelina was quick to respond. "There was the woman who had the notebook on every issue that could come up in a meeting. Oh, no— closer still, there was that video guy, the one with the maintenance company."

"Steve Ray. He talked about seeing each person's potential. And I don't think I mentioned this before, but something else Ray said comes back to me:

"I hire people I can reward."

"Hire people to reward. Prepare for every meeting by considering whom you can recognize. Same continuum. Steve Ray has reached the level of gifted boss because he's realized that he can spend his time either correcting mistakes, or applauding victories. Which would you rather do?

"And Shane Evangelist has become the jewel of the company's young executives because he's realized he can either spend his time trying to impress people, or trying to help them. Remember him on the airplane moving from first class into a coach seat? Why? To discuss a younger man's future. You do that, and whenever you're going into a meeting with that young man, you understand him, probably better than anyone else in the meeting. That's how you get your third eye working: You let the light of knowledge in and then it comes back out as awareness."

Our food arrived and we ate for a while, each lost in our thoughts and plans. Eventually I said, "Here's what I'm thinking. Like most everybody else, when I start feeling ambitious, I try to get ahead and impress people by working harder. And working harder works—my bosses are grateful. Fine. However, the level of effort in our company is pretty high—there are a lot of people working very hard and doing more of their work than they have to. We're all trying to be different by doing more of the same. But what if I spent those extra hours doing *different* work? Like the Blockbuster guy—*he doesn't just work a lot, he does work nobody else does, like spending time before a meeting thinking through the needs of everyone who'll be there."*

Angelina understood and pointed at me with the taco she was holding, and said, "Instead of being another nice person who works hard, he made himself special by doing special work."

"I don't suppose there are that many people who are truly unique," I replied. "It's like that line—'You are a one-of-a-kind individual, just like everyone else'—but you don't need any special genetic gifts to figure how to make a unique contribution. You start by figuring out what the usual contribution is, and then make yours different.

"Which takes us right back to the jump in logic: *Here's what's expected. Now, what else can we do?*"

Max sat, barely moving, not wanting to interrupt our revelations; he'd even pulled his lips in and chewed on them to keep from jumping in. We both looked at him, waiting for the burst of confirmation that is one of the things that makes Max special. He shifted his eyes back and forth, waiting to make certain we were through. And then let out a sputter of enthusiasm saying,

"I'm just sitting here watching lights come on, like I'm in Sausalito at dusk, looking out at San Francisco."

He later added, "Of all the people I asked about their better-than-perfect colleagues, *not one* spoke about a genius who was smarter than anyone else. *Not one* spoke about patents or engineering or programming. Instead, they all talked about people who had some special understanding or insight. They described people with a hyper-awareness of others.

"They did not describe people who are better than they are, they described people who made them feel better about themselves.

"And that's good news for us all, because that is a skill we all can learn. And, as I sat here, eating excellent carnitas, I got to hear two people explain exactly how it's done. A toast to two jewels."

The Sales Job of the Century

After we'd eaten and were having coffee, Max told us a story about a man who took it upon himself to change the course of science and history, and who, despite being a scientist, and not a salesman, managed to sell a billion-dollar project. Notice in the story how he shrewdly built a jump into hyper-logic.

"Have you been following the Human Genome Project?" Max asked by way of introduction. He didn't wait for an answer.

"The media has apparently lost interest, but it remains one of the great human undertakings. It's the biomedical equivalent of building the Transcontinental Railroad, the step that will carry progress along its tracks.

"And like the railroad, it wasn't that the idea was inconceivable—other railroads had been built—rather, it was a project so vast it was almost impossible to conceive of anyone pulling it off.

"Which brings us to Charles DeLisi. He'd been at the National Institute of Health for a decade, working in cellular immunology— whatever that is. During that time, he'd considered whether the human genome sequencing would ever be done. He'd toss the idea out to colleagues and get a response he labeled 'polite indifference.' It was too vast a project to waste intellectual capital trying to envision.

"Then, after he'd moved over to the Department of Energy, he read a report that mentioned the idea of doing the entire genome sequencing. His reaction was, '*So I'm not the only one in the world!*' And this emboldened him to convene a conference to discuss the idea. The reception was lukewarm. One of the people DeLisi most wanted to attend turned him down, saying, 'I don't want to spin my wheels.' Still, by convening the conference, he had found a core of fellow believers.

"Next, DeLisi took it upon himself to sell an idea that would require a billion dollars and nearly two decades to complete. Sell it to whom? It was too vast a project for NIH, and it didn't really fit DOE; plus, he'd have to convince the Office of Management of the Budget to allocate the money. In other words, he needed to sell the scientific community (many of whom felt that the investment was so large it would siphon funds from their own endeavors) while selling thre giant government agencies. Impossible, right?

"Well, they say fools rush in, and they also say angels go where mortals fear to tread. Maybe DeLisi was a foolhardy angel, but he took on the task. It wasn't his job, but he took it on anyway.

"He told me, 'I like to talk to people and so I went around and infiltrated the community.' Interesting verb for him to choose: *infiltrated*. And he found a Senator—Domenici of New Mexico—to help with Congress. As for selling it to the agencies that would have to be responsible for the project, guess how he sold them?"

"By figuring out what they needed," Angelina said confidently.

"Bingo. He knew that the DOE was accustomed to taking on giant engineering projects, but not giant science projects. So he sold it as an engineering project, making clear to them that it had 'a beginning, a middle, and an end.' He laid out the entire project, making an impossibly massive task seem doable, bit by bit, year by year.

"He also said proudly that the OMB responded to his proposal by telling him, 'It makes more sense than most things we see.'

"He spoke to engineers in engineering terms, accountants in dollars, and scientists about how it would promote their own their endeavors, and, whenever necessary, he bypassed professional logic and went right to the emotions. He'd carry with him a list of genetic disorders that would, one day, by eliminated via gene replacement. And he had video footage of sufferers of Huntington's Chorea, a disease arising from a single gene that causes those who have it lose motor control—the word 'chorea' is from the same root as 'choreography'—so you can imagine the power of that film."

Max paused to let us imagine, and I have to say that I'm grateful DeLisi knew what he was doing.

"So what can we learn?" Max soon asked.

I gave it a shot: "It wasn't his job—it wasn't anyone's job—and so it was not a reasonable undertaking. So it fits our first premise.

"Next, no one asked him to be a hero, but he became one by asking lots of other people to be heroes. How could you hear his pitch and see his video and say no? You can't say no, because he wasn't asking you for money or approval, he was asking you to be part of one of the world's great undertakings. So he had the sexy brain working.

"Finally, he spoke to his audiences in their own jargon—whether engineering, biology, politics, or bureaucracy—as well as in the universal language of emotion. He didn't ask for help; he offered you a piece of what you went into government work in order to achieve, a chance to make a contribution to the public good. That's how he paired a brain throb with an organizational third eye."

———————————

Angelina pulled together a conclusion, saying, "He was lovably unreasonable, added to the giant brain by making everyone dream, then closed the loop by speaking to each person's needs, including in his case the universal need for significance."

Theatrically, Max brought his arm up, then slapped the table and declared victory.

The Art of Being Beloved

I'd succeeded in beating Max to a check for once, and we were driving back across town to the hotel when Max pointed out the value to our careers of becoming skilled loop-closers.

"We know we have to use the third eye to see the loop others don't," Max instructed us. "Imagine if you could do that when you're up for a new job.

"This is another case where Connie Mariano's example teaches us. You remember my saying that her boss nominated her for the job at the White House, even though she wasn't certain she could do it. But once she was in the running, she *ran*.

"She had to face a series of interviews, with the chief one being with the man she eventually replaced. And instead of just working on trying to impress him with talk of herself, she...." He stopped himself. "Guess what's next."

"She studied the people who'd interview her," Angelina said.

"Precisely. In her case, it was basically one man who'd make the decision. She went into that meeting not only ready to talk about her strengths, but knowing his. She knew what he valued, and how he talked about teamwork and sacrifice, and what he called 'the servant mentality.' She got in the interview, and used his own words with him, and halfway through he stood up, went out to his assistant, and said, 'Cancel the rest of the interviews—we have our person.'"

Max looked at me and even in the darkness of the car, I could see his hammy squint of inquiry. "I know what you're thinking," he said. Still, he waited till I asked him, "But what if the person you're meeting isn't famous, with a public record of interviews or articles?"

"Everybody is famous—at some level. You might find trade press articles, you might meet people who worked with the person, or know him or her through an association. If nothing else, you ask."

The next point, Max informed us, was to see how closing the loop can make you 'beloved.' Here he had a case study from Taser

International—you know, the Taser gun people. Here's how he put it.

"I asked their chairman about best-ever colleagues, and one that he raved about was the company's CFO, who was promoted to COO. The chairman is Phil Smith, who looks like he should be a senator—a stately man with a twinkle in his eye. And, boy, did he go into high twinkle when he talked about Kathy Hanrahan, the CFO-turned-COO.

"When the company was getting ready to go public, the big accounting firm that was handling the public offering told Phil to go out and hire himself a 'name brand' CFO, someone the Wall Street folks would trust. Phil's response was quite candid: 'You're full of...' well, let's just say, full of 'bleep.' He trusted her completely and so did their executives and suppliers.

"Being trusted by the suppliers was no simple matter, because early in Taser's history, they'd had a long financial drought, and there were vendors who didn't get paid for nine months. *Nine months.* Even so, Phil says, 'Not one of them deserted us. They love her. They knew she would never lie to them. And she understood that people will walk through fire with you, if you communicate.'

"Then he told me his theory of fire-walk communication. He said:

"The best thing you can give people is, of course, good news. Second best is bad news. By far the worst is no news."

"Kathy understands that. With me and everyone else, you get information before you have to ask.'"

Max slapped the steering wheel. "There it is again—that word *before*." Wound up by the thought, he said, "If you're one of the better-than-perfect people, you know what questions are going to be asked before the meeting starts. You know what impresses people before the interview starts. You know the step beyond the next logical step. You have an information periscope and can see around the corners."

"But," I said tentatively, "when is it too much information? Won't people see through you and resent the private eye stuff?"

Max thought for so long that I wondered if he was starting to nap. It was late, after all, and he'd just eaten. Since he was driving, these worries had me leaning over, prepared to grab the wheel. Eventually he noticed and slapped my hand away, saying, "I'm on top of things. I'm taking your question seriously. I'm trying to think of a case of that happening. I'm getting the opposite conclusion from every example I can recall.

"For one, remember me telling you about the high-priced executive coach, Steve Hardison? When I asked him about the colleague who'd meant the most to him in his career, he couldn't give enough praise to a guy who ran a tech company. He was crazy about this guy. He said, 'I went to an interview and knew I wanted to work for him. He asked me what I needed to be paid and I told him, 'I don't care.' And I meant it. I would have worked for him for free.'"

"How did *that* work?" I asked, and Max came back with a little four-word quote from Hardison: "I felt his depth." I wasn't certain I knew what it meant, but I agreed that I'd like to be thought of as deep. (Although I confess that I wondered if my yearning to be thought of as deep wasn't an especially shallow reaction.)

Max cut short my self-doubts by saying, "After being there a while and becoming a star employee, the boss said to Steve one day, 'I work with you; I ought to understand who you are.' Well, Steve is a Mormon, and seriously so. So this busy CEO tells Steve to buy them tickets to a BYU football game and that they'll fly there for the weekend. He even says, 'Take me to the temple and show me your world.' Not because he wanted a new faith or a church, but just to better understand a great employee. Think of that: Most people see two guys in white shirts and ties on bicycles and then pull the drapes and pretend they aren't home, but this guy was flying to BYU and going to the temple.

"So," Max said, shrugging, "is that private eye stuff? I can only tell you that two decades after it happened, Steve Hardison told me with a thick voice that he studied his boss and 'felt his depth.' So what do you suppose depth is?"

I was pleased that Angelina responded from the back seat, "Curiosity. His depth was how deeply he learned about the people around him."

A Unified Theory

"Give her a high five for me," Max said, thumping on dashboard for emphasis. "And now we have brought together our topics and fit them into one unified theory:

> *"Best-ever colleagues think differently because they know more. They know more because they've asked more."*

A Thousand Eyes

We pulled into the hotel parking lot, and the valet hustled out to take Max's rental car. We stood in the warm desert air, none of us wanting to go back to our rooms, but each of us knowing that we had early flights.

"One last point and I'm going to bed," Max said. "I came across a number of examples of how people increased their ability to close the loop by having more people contribute to their ability to see and understand. We talked before of adding brain lobes. This time we should think of adding contributors to the third-eye vision. One of the reasons that people who are passionate about their work tend to do well is that passion is an idea magnet. Take me, for instance. What do you know that I'm passionate about?" he asked me.

"Life? Shakespeare? Corny jokes?"

"There you go. People send me funny jokes—they save them for me; I have become a depository, a ..."

"A recycling center?"

Max took a playful swat at my head and I leaned sideways to let it pass by.

"Let's move onto Shakespeare before I get any more abuse. People call me and say, 'Did you hear about the new *Macbeth* coming to town?' Or they send me a new DVD, or clip an article. Their eyes are my eyes because they know of my passion. And it's no different in business. So a person who loves new technology will have extra eyes, and a person who loves ideas will see them, remotely, through the eyes of others. People love to be the eyes of others, and it brings them closer to you. That's why it's important to have a passion and to let it show.

How the RV Got a New Bed

"Say you have a passion for better customer service. Bill McLaughlin, CEO of Select Comfort—do you know who I mean?"

"The Sleep Number Bed people," Angelina answered.

"Yes. Their CEO sends a weekly voice mail to everyone in the company, mostly talking about better service. And using a telephone system called In-Touch, he is able to get responses from employees—direct to his ear, no middleman.

"Getting fresh information is difficult. As another executive once told me, she wanted to get comments 'with the exclamation point still attached.' That's what McLaughlin gets. Sure, he gets complaints, but they are the kind he wants, like when they instituted a 30-day return policy. One clerk let him know that he had just killed their Christmas sales of pillows and bedding, because those gift items are often purchased more than a month out. The policy was instantly revoked.

"But here's the story I wanted to get to. I love this. One employee left him a message one day saying, 'I just had a woman in here who loves her Sleep Number bed so much she wants to put one in her RV.' So the company contacted Winnebago and now the beds are being offered in high-end models. That employee called because she wanted to share her pleasure at seeing such a happy customer. McLaughlin's passion let him receive and put that story to use."

Max gave me another of his looks as though he was offended that I wasn't more excited by the story. "You're thinking that you can't apply that idea, right?"

"Just the opposite. I was thinking I could use one of those little handheld recorders when I'm out meeting with customers. When I hear something useful, I could ask them to put it on tape. They'd be flattered, and I could play them at our meetings and let everyone hear what they say. It's one thing to tell people what a customer said; it's another to play it for them. It would be especially good as a way to honor the support people who came through for them."

One for the Record Book

Max massaged my shoulder and my ego, then grinned at Angelina and said to her, "Now this suggestion is for you, because it sounds like your office could use an energy injection and you are the one to bring the syringe. What I want for you, Angelina, is to become the office expert on excellence. Here's a case study to illustrate how you do it.

"Mark Ferguson runs the New Mexico division of D.R. Horton, now the leading homebuilder in the country. We came up with an idea for him, whereby he'd create a record book for his group. They started assembling stats on 'most closings in a month' and so on—the obvious records. But then they started looking for other items to include, to bring in more types of employees. One of them was an astounding feat involving what they call 'zero-defect walks.'

"This is where you do the 'walk-though' to inspect your house, and you make a 'punch-list' of all that's wrong. Well, it turned out that one of their supervisors had done seven 'zero-defect walks' in a row. Seven times the customer had walked out with nothing wrong. Amazing. How did he do it? He'd developed a system and it worked. He was an instant star.

"As more records were noted, the meetings and staff reports started to sound like the Sports page instead of the Business section. Who's working on a record? Whose string is in jeopardy? Now eyes are open and ideas are flying around as people try to help each other."

Angelina nodded. "I can see just how to do it. And I can see what you mean about energy. I'd love to be setting records. I think of how hard I go to try to set a personal best on the treadmill at the gym—that's the sort of zest I'd like to bring to my work."

The New Deal

No one wanted to leave and so we talked for another hour, standing in the courtyard. We understood that we now had a mutual passion—searching for 'perfects' to surpass—and that we'd be sharing stories, ideas, and records. But we also learned from Max that we'd be sharing a trip to Hawaii.

"This speech that you've helped me with is shaping up nicely," Max began. "It's only right that you two be there. It's a month from tomorrow and, if you can get off work, I want to bring you with me to Maui. I'd like to fob off the speaking on you two, but I can't figure out how to do it. I still want you there. So, here's the plan: a long weekend in Maui, on me, as thanks for your inspiration, guidance, and research. Deal?"

Max's Speech

Dare to be naïve.

—Buckminster Fuller

*My best friend is the one who brings out
the best in me.*

—Henry Ford

———————————————

We met Max at a sprawling resort in Maui, and the environment was, of course, stimulating in a relaxing way—if you've visited any tropical island, you know what I mean.

The speech was to a group of marketing executives and their spouses. I figured out pretty quickly that the event was not worth all of Max's planning and research, and I then tumbled to the conclusion that he'd known as much all along—he was just using the speech as an excuse to involve us in his endless curiosity.

Let me recount the speech for you, as it served as a summing-up of all we'd learned together. Many of the examples Max used, were, of course, ones we have discussed, so I will cut in to summarize those for you.

First, the scene: It was a dressy affair, by Hawaiian standards—lots of beautiful linens and silk. There were 40 or 50 tables, each with a floral centerpiece and candles, lending a pastel glow, so the room embraced you like a soft, yellow robe.

The man who introduced Max was self-important and long-winded, but it allowed the audience to settle in. There was a sweet moment when they called Max up to have a medal placed around his neck. He bounced across the stage, wearing linen trousers with a pale green guayebera—one of those shirts you see on Latin gentlemen—and, of course, his signature bolo tie, this one with a round silver clasp. The woman doing the placing of the medal was about half Max's height, and he clowned around, bowing theatrically, arms outstretched.

Then when Max returned to his full height and faced the audience, those of us who knew Max let out a howl of delight, for someone had turned the medal into a bolo tie.

Then it was Max's turn to speak. He sauntered across the stage to a rosewood lectern, the stage empty, a blue curtain behind him. He left the medal on, re-clipping the wireless microphone to it so his hands were as free as they were empty—no notes. He stood for a moment, gathering himself, then began.

"Someone once sent me a romance ad from a newspaper. It was one of those that had a section called 'ME' followed by one called 'YOU.' The 'ME' section had a long list of adjectives:

ME: athletic, lively, outgoing, affluent, cultured, generous and stimulating.

"That was followed by the second section, which consisted of just two words:

YOU: grateful.

"That graceful word *grateful* applies in three ways this evening. One, I am grateful for the honor you have presented me with tonight. Two, I am grateful for two special people in the audience."

He forced Angelina and me to stand, telling everyone that we were the ones who'd inspired the research and, to hear him tell it, the authors of everything he was about to say.

"Finally, I am grateful for all the colleagues—bosses, employees, suppliers, and customers—who have made me better at what I do. They did so by truly encouraging me, not with mere praise, but by pushing and pulling me. They could have told me that my work was perfect and let me be content. Instead, they forced me to be better.

"I'd like to invite each of you to consider the best colleague you've ever had, the one person you'd choose to work with again, if you could pick just one. I'll wait a minute and let you mentally picture that person."

It's always tricky to ask an audience that has been eating and drinking to turn contemplative, but, as I looked around, I could see smiles appear, and a murmur started as husbands and wives asked each other who it was the other was thinking of. Eventually Max cut into the chatting, and we were surprised to see that he'd stepped down off the stage and was among the tables.

"If you're not grinning, then you're not doing it right." He pointed at some people grinning and nodded at them in understanding.

Then he asked for examples. The most memorable was an M.D. who ran a radiology clinic. "That means," the doctor explained to us, "I work in a place where we hurt people to help them."

He then said, he voice thickening at the recollection:

> *"We have a nurse who works there who is brutally efficient but lovably kind. She asked me one day if she could hang a bell in the waiting room. We always say that she's an angel, and there's that thing from the movie 'It's A Wonderful Life' about when you hear a bell an angel gets his or her wings—still, I was hesitant.*

She promised me that I'd like it but after a week, if I didn't, she'd take it down."

She had, of course, sold the idea by selling an experiment. But wait to you hear what that little bell did.

"She hung up the bell—it was perhaps 4 inches high, with a little nylon cord on the clapper—basically a dinner bell. Then she started telling clients that, when they finished their course of treatment, they were to ring the bell to signify their victory.

"Well, the trial week came and went and I would have punched anyone who tried to take down that stupid bell. Whenever we heard it, everyone in the waiting room would cheer, and the whole staff would run out front to congratulate the person. And the other patients would see that and it became a kind of calendar: 'Two weeks till I ring the bell!'

"One day I realized the right word for the response to the bell: gleeful. In an office of sick and scared people,

we now have moments of glee. And it made everyone want more of them.

"Now we have dozens of special days, like when we all dress as one of the Marx Brothers. It's silly, but it helps. And I believe that our patients do better because of it. We are trying to help them live, and we made our office into a place full of life."

A number of people in the audience teared up at the story, and Max gently let the nurse and bell take him into the next section of his speech.

"Isn't it fitting that that moving story ended with the words *full of life*. Isn't that the mark of the best people and the best places? Let's consider people in the workplace who are *full of life*. Let's start by compiling a list of the characteristics of a great leader. It's a familiar list: honorable, intelligent, compassionate, open-minded, decisive, and, of course, highly competent.

"Now, here's where it gets intriguing. Consider the items in that list of leadership traits and consider this: Which ones would you *remove* if asked the traits of, say, the ideal engineer or great customer service rep?

"Okay, which would you remove in defining a great supplier? A great customer? Or, for that matter, a great friend or spouse?"

Max waited, pretending it was not a rhetorical question. No one offered any candidates for removal.

"If you're like me, you wouldn't remove any. And I don't believe there's a need to add any, either, because we are describing the best of what it means to be human. When I interviewed people at all levels about their best-ever colleagues, what I heard were stories about the best in human nature, stories that happened to be set in the workplace.

"The upshot is this:

> *"If you want to learn to be a better boss, learn to be a better customer."*

> *"If you want to learn to be a better employee, learn to be a better boss."*

> *"If you want to learn to be a better supplier, learn to be a better friend."*

"The skills are interchangeable, because they are the skills of tapping into the best of being human."

Now he paused, as if a new thought had just occurred to him, switching into a voice of sighing compassion.

"There is a marvelous Hindu story of a prince who was kidnapped by bandits as a young child. He is raised by these bandits and becomes a skilled and ruthless highwayman, one who knows no other life and remembers nothing of his royal birth.

"One day, plying his disreputable trade, he surprises the spiritual advisor to the King. The guru sees in the bandit's face the King's adolescent face, realizes who the boy must be, and says with deep tenderness, 'Your Royal Highness.' The young man scoffs in response."

Returning to the lectern, Max brought a small sheet of paper from his pocket and unfolded it.

"Here's the denouement of that story, in the words of the marvelous writer, Eknath Easwaran:

> *The spiritual teacher goes up to the young man, puts his arm around him, and begins to tell him stories about his childhood—how his father used to carry him on his shoulders, how his mother used to sing him to sleep, how his life was in the palace.*

'Gradually the prince begins to remember. He says, 'Go, on, go on!' The spiritual teacher goes on relating anecdotes of his royal childhood. Finally the young man says, 'Now I recall.' And the young prince goes home to his father, the king.'

"As we search for people who make organizations special, we realize that they do so because *they* are special. They are the ones who *recall.* They have gifts we all have—the jewels of humanity—but they are special because they have remembered to use them. They aren't stuck trying to perfect some role given them by society; they are explorers, pioneers on the frontier of recollection."

———————

Max waited, taking a drink of bottled water, before changing tempos and topics, moving more quickly now.

"Enough philosophy, let's get practical. I want to tell you about three ways that great colleagues are profoundly different from typical professionals.

"They are lovably unreasonable.

"They have sexy brains, ones that attract other brains.

"And they have an uncanny awareness of the communication needs of others, an organizational third eye.

"Said another way—they think, learn, and relate differently than most of us. Any one of the three makes a person special; all three make them seem as though they come from a higher-order species.

"Our friend with the bell is an example of the defining trait of the people who think differently: They are lovably unreasonable. Think about it for a minute: A bell in a radiology clinic? Is that reasonable? Is that logical? Only after the fact. And is that even part of a nurse's job description, bell installation? No, it isn't.

"But she wasn't being a perfect nurse—she was after something more. To get there, she had to leave behind nurse logic and leap to another level of service, what is akin to jumping to warp-speed, or what some of us like to call hyper-logic. One-three-two.

"As you listened to that story, I think you understand why I have come to think of these human gems as *better than perfect*. By doing more than their jobs, they are the true creators of the culture, the ones who lift those around them."

Max gave more 'unreasonable' examples, including:

> Clients—both the rock star who became a typist for the day, and the woman from Levi's who asked for better ways to pass along information.
>
> An employee—the woman whose budget for a new "concierge" service initiative got wiped out and she did it anyway.
>
> A boss—the military doctor who sent his star employee to the White House even when she doubted herself.
>
> Businesses—including the packaging company that built in innovations and celebrated them with its five team Final Four, and the furniture store with same-day delivery.

"These represent a different way of thinking," Max continued. "You can't get to those conclusions by doing the reasonable, logical thing. You can't get there by perfecting how you work. These are examples of those who are more kind or courageous or stubborn than a reasonable person would be.

"Can you look back and say of their actions, 'Well, it worked out for them and it even ended up being in their self-interest'? Yes. They have hindsight while the rest of us are still squinting ahead. They don't ask what's up ahead at the intersection; they've already driven down the next street and sent back their reconnaissance. And what is the knowledge they send back? Simply this: You never know. Something wonderful is out there, and we need to take a shot at it.

"The Keepers of Consistency—by which I mean most bankers, investors, managers, and executives—crave certainty, but what they need is a bit of you-never-know. Where there is certainty, there is no discovery. Where there is certainty, there are no heroes."

Max let that one hang in the air, and strolled back to the lectern to get a drink from a bottle of water. It didn't seem like we were listening to a speech; it seemed like we were sitting in the library of a wise man as he paced and mused.

He ran his hand through his thinning white hair and turned to us as though he has just thought of something else to let us in on.

"One of the saddest business stories I've heard in recent years came from a book about the JCPenney Company. The founder, James Cash Penney, was an admirable man who built an exceptional organization, in large part by giving store managers freedom to experiment, turning the chain into a series of retail laboratories.

"But let me get to the sad part. Until the day he died, James Cash Penney took pride in his tidy appearance, and he always bragged that his suits were Penney's brand, Towncraft, right off the rack. I hate to tell you this, but *that was not true*.

"Unbeknownst to him, his suits were custom-made and then the Towncraft labels were sewn in to fool him and the public. Why? Because the handlers around him felt that he no longer looked right in a suit, because he had become pear-shaped and a difficult fit.

"The truth was that JCPenney's did not make suits to fit Mr. Penney. So they deceived him. Doing so, they lost not only honor, but also creativity.

"Fear of the truth is a learning shield. If they had embraced the facts, they might have come up with a line of specialty suits. Perhaps they would have done the same with women, and perhaps they would have beaten the retail chain Chico's—one of the hottest retailers around—to the conclusion that the old sizing templates didn't work any longer. Penney's missed the market because they feared the truth.

"On the other hand, the colleagues that we celebrate here today are not only interested in the truth, but they are intensely curious about new truths and new people. They understand that knowing people with ideas that are different from their own is a way to increase their knowledge base.

"Our better-than-perfect colleagues build big, throbbing, connected brains—they have a human version of the Internet available to them. When faced with an undertaking, they don't issue orders; they ask questions. This means they don't just call on their own experience or wisdom, but on the great wisdom of the giant brain."

———————————

Max then offered as an example the young star of Blockbuster and how he engaged the team brain to drop the time it takes to process an order below the level he'd dared hoped for. Max then went on to talk about other ways of learning—by experimenting and by welcoming criticism. He spoke of the church that couldn't be great, so it just did good instead, starting with a small project. Then he talked of Frank Gehry, who was "such a genius that he'd tear up his work and do it over, knowing it would be better." He did not mention the 80/20 Approach—which was a shame, because I've tried passing along projects and it's a powerful approach to engaging the big brain. He did, however, mention the gear manufacturer with the atrium art gallery and the $50 shoe samples.

Max finished up the section by walking out into the audience once again.

"You know the old expression 'heart throb?' It means someone who is so romantically attractive that your heat beats faster. Like Ralph here."

Max stood behind the organization's president and put his hands on the man's shoulders.

Simultaneously, I felt Angelina's hand on my forearm and I thought she was going to whisper a compliment to me, but she was merely leveraging herself up to get a look at the guy. And, yes, he was one of those young-old swells, like Bill Clinton.

"However, instead of a heart throb, the colleagues I've studied were brain throbs. They have sexy brains. They make your brain twitch because you know they will tell you something new or ask you something different. They seek out the unexpected and are carriers of the curiosity virus."

Max strolled across the room, letting the silence build curiosity. Then he eased into the third section.

"'You never have to ask.'

"That little compliment was one we heard often in our research. You never have to ask. Why? Because while perfect colleagues ask the right questions, the better-than-perfect colleagues have already asked enough questions to know what you want and need, and to have come back with even better questions for you."

Max went on to talk about the woman at Taser and the three levels of news—good, bad, and none. He also described the Blockbuster executive moving to the back of the airplane to discuss a younger associate's career, along with the bureaucracy-leaping phone system used by the Sleep Number Bed folks. Next, he told us the story of Charles DeLisi, the man who sold the billion-dollar human genome project. He came up with a new angle to that story, worth passing along.

———————

"What Dr. DeLisi did was sell the dream as he sold the practical possibility. He sold the science, the engineering, and the politics, adjusting his pitch to the ears of each audience. He didn't just tell a story; he told *the* story that each audience needed to hear. How did he know? He asked.

"And so we get to see how it all fits together. He did an unreasonable thing, taking on a project no one assigned him. It wasn't in his, or anyone else's, job description. It was not a logical undertaking, but he made it his. One, three, two.

"He started by asking questions, by engaging others. He was a carrier of curiosity. And then he gave back that curiosity with a third-eye vision of what was needed.

"He didn't just have a plan. He didn't just have a dream. He had a story, and he gave everyone who heard it a role to play in that story. He wasn't just a hero; he was a maker of heroes."

The crowd was moved by that one, and Max let them contemplate it as he walked back up the steps to the stage. He'd passed his allotted speaking time by that point, and he said so. Someone yelled out, "Keep going. Take your time." Others shouted out their agreement. Max grinned at them and took out a handkerchief and passed it over his forehead. That's when I noticed that he had a good sweat going; he was giving us every bit of energy in that old lion's body.

"You are kind. But I am near the end. As you have no doubt figured out on your own, the ideas I am relating today are inter-related. Great colleagues think differently because they've learned and communicated more. But there's one thing I don't want to leave out. These people make organizations better because they are better people.

"They aren't just good; they make everyone better. Their joy is our joy, and that's the best working definition of friendship that I've encountered.

"What men! What women! What friends! If you are the sort of person to seek out new ideas, no matter where they are found or in whom, you are *open-minded*. If you are experimenting and learning, you are *courageous*. If you seek to understand while knowing that you can never get to the end of it, you are *compassionate*. If you give without being asked, you are *generous*.

"So let's take a look at those four virtues: open-minded, courageous, compassionate, and generous. Add them together and you get an old-fashioned virtue, that of being *noble*.

"The people who make an organization special are the organizational nobles, embracing those who carry us, leaping, into the future. Are they perfect? Yes. And then they change, surprising us again and again. They are better than perfect."

Max bowed slightly, and we knew he had finished. Still, the audience waited, hoping for more. When he turned to walk off, the crowd rose; everyone in the room was eager to be the first to start the standing ovation.

Afterword

You might want to stop reading right there, with Max's speech. However, it occurred to me that perhaps you'd like to know what became of Angelina and me after our trip to Hawaii and Max's speech.

First off, Max persuaded me to write this book. He doesn't have the patience for writing, but he knew we were on to something important, worthy of passing along to you, good reader.

Coming back from our trip, I certainly felt we had it all figured out, but I wasn't so sure

181

after the first couple of months. I'll explain that in a minute, but first let me give you an update on Angelina.

She went back and undertook the creation of a company record book. It went over big. She started sending out updates, and lots of people were eager to play in that game of records. The project put her in touch with all the people in the company doing exceptional work, and she became Dream Central for the high achievers. One of the VPs spotted this and had the HR folks create a position of Excellence Guru. Odd title, in my opinion, but the effect was something special for Angelina, as she was sent to visit companies doing amazing things to help their employees, and from those ideas invented better ones for her company. So she's suddenly the liaison between top management and top performers. She put herself smack in the middle of the company's energy flow and its future.

The only downside is that I don't see her as much—all the travel. But she's happier, and knows she made a connection between her best self and her work. It shows up in her personal life, as well, now that she no longer spends part of each day wondering what she's missing out on. As for spilling over into her personal life, she finally stopped wondering about me, and we set a date to get married. It worked out that we're going back to the same resort in Maui, a week and a year after Max's speech there.

———————————

As for me, I came back eager to work on my 'organizational third eye' and started seeking out people doing interesting work. I discovered we had quite a few jewels in and around our company. The level of conversation is different with these folks—they love to discuss problems and solutions. When they meet there's an understanding there in the room (as Max would say) that whoever has the most intriguing problem wins, because they all want to pitch in and help that person jump to hyper-logic. Further, by looking for better-than-perfect colleagues, I began looking at myself differently, trying to live up.

Max sent me a copy of the letters of Seneca, with some passages marked, including this one:

> [Your] personality should be provided with someone it can revere... Happy the man who improves other people not merely when he is in their presence but even when he is in their thoughts! And happy, too, is the person who can revere another so as to adjust and shape his own

> *personality in the light of recollections*
> *of that other. A person able to revere*
> *another thus will soon deserve to be*
> *revered himself.*

However, while I was learning by example, there was a hitch—a big one. I started talking up the idea of welcoming challenges, and the next thing I knew—bang—one of the senior guys had dumped on me his nightmare project, working with a demanding jerk of a client.

I immediately called Max, to rib him about his techniques having stuck me with a quagmire of an undertaking, and he responded, as I should have guessed, "I wonder what an anti-quagmire device would look like. Whoever built one would be quite the hero, eh?"

So, with much sighing and self-pity, I decided to make the best of it. I realized that the other people at our firm who'd worked with the 'jerk' had mostly avoided him. I decided to understand him. After a couple of meetings, I told him that it would help me if I could come along with him on some undertaking he found meaningful. (I was thinking of Max's story of the boss going to the BYU game with his Mormon employee.) My client took me to a shooting range. I've never wanted anything to do with guns, so this was a burden. But I went and I saw him relax, and we had some laughs. A week later he took me skeet shooting, which I actually enjoyed.

You're probably wanting to jump in with, "The point?"

Well, I'm still no gun lover, but I did learn a bit and, when it was time to contemplate together what his new office building would be like, I brought to the meeting two rifles: a cheap, utilitarian one, and a collector's item, a gorgeous reproduction of a gun given to Wild Bill Hickock.

You can picture how that conversation went: I asked him if he wanted to do the cheapest per-square-foot route, or the create-something-marvelous route. We ended up asking ourselves *"How wonderful could it be?"*

The cynics at the office were amazed with what we came up with, and how the budget was far larger than anyone would have believed. We created a modern building with some nods to the Old West, including some design items inspired by gun metal, along with a little Boot Hill, where old products and bad ideas are given burial ceremonies, and a 'saloon' where employees can have a drink and have 'idea gun fights.'

Two things happened in my career because of that victory. I now get all the company's 'unreasonable' clients and that's fine with me—

most of them just want to be treated as someone special—and I believe every one of them is just that. How do I know how all those clients want to be treated? I ask. The second thing that happened is that I'm sent out to meet with clients who want something new and different, which is just where I want to work.

So, what can we learn?

Taking Angelina's experience and mine together, I can see now that we have specialized in thinking, learning, and communicating differently. This is what leads you to have an organizational third eye and sexy brain, and thereby come up with lovably unreasonable endeavors. Try it. Start with something that's 'perfect' and make it better.

With that, we come full circle, and you can appreciate the quote from Jonathan Swift that I chose for us to begin with: "May you live all the days of your life." Those who devote themselves to being better than perfect know just how that feels, just as they know that every day is a chance to ask:

How wonderful could it be?

Acknowledgments and Sources

The marvelous echoing question, "How wonderful could it be?" came from a film documentary about the director Michael Tilson Thomas called *Keeping Store*. You can buy it at the San Francisco Symphony's Online store and I can't recommend it too highly—it is a brain throb journey with a better-than-perfect performer.

Books I mentioned in the text that you might want details on: *Wooster Proposes, Jeeves Disposes* by Kristin Thompson is from James Heineman publishing. The A.A. Milne novel discussed in the text is *The Red House Mystery*—the version I have is from 2003 from Wildside Press. The story about John Cash Penney came from *Celebration of Fools: An Inside Look at The Rise and Fall of JCPenney* by Bill Hare, published by Amacom.

Nearly all of the other stories in the book came from my interviews with the people quoted. I am grateful for their time and willingness to join our circle of helping.

This book also benefited from the aide and counsel of a number of better-than-perfect colleagues. In addition to those quoted in the text, I am thankful for the help of Janet Traylor, Bobette Gorden, Steve Brown, Bob Cialdini, Connie Denk, Paula Wigboldy, Joel Dauten, and Sandy Dauten, as well as the good people at Career Press, and my friends at King Features and at the Innovators' Lab.

About the Author

Dale Dauten has been researching achievers and innovation since his time as a graduate student at Stanford University's Graduate School of Business. His early work prompted a government publication to call him a "guru" to White House staffers and, since then, his books been published in a dozen languages and have developed a worldwide following, especially in Japan.

As founder of The Innovators Lab, Dale has done idea-generation work with dozens of firms, including Georgia-Pacific, United Auto Group, General Dynamics, Caterpillar, and NASA.

He also writes two newspaper columns, both nationally syndicated by King Features: *The Corporate Curmudgeon* and *Kate and Dale Talk Jobs* (with employment expert Kate Wendleton). His work appears weekly in more than 100 newspapers nationally.

Dale lives in Tempe, Arizona, with his wife and three children.

Other works by Dale Dauten include:
  The Max Strategy
  The Gifted Boss
  The Laughing Warriors

For information on *Better than Perfect* speeches and seminars, please visit *www.dauten.com*.

Dale also welcomes your comments and experiences: *dale@dauten.com*.